To LeRoy
from Dale
Happy Easter 1991

D1550930

Walt Disney

and
Assorted
Other
Characters

Walt Disney
and
Assorted
Other
Characters

An Unauthorized
Account of
the Early Years
at Disney's

by

JACK KINNEY

Foreword
by Leonard Maltin

Harmony Books/New York

Dedicated to those artists who worked in the trenches
during the Golden Age of Animation

Copyright © 1988 by Jack Kinney

All rights reserved. No part of this book may be
reproduced or transmitted in any form or by any
means, electronic or mechanical, including
photocopying, recording, or by any information
storage and retrieval system, without permission in
writing from the publisher.
Published by Harmony Books, a division of Crown
Publishers, Inc., 225 Park Avenue South, New
York, New York 10003
HARMONY and colophon are trademarks of Crown
Publishers, Inc.
Manufactured in the United States of America

Design by Debra Elliot Bennett
Art Restoration by Pepé Moreno

Library of Congress Cataloging-in-Publication Data

Kinney, Jack.
   Walt Disney and assorted other characters : an
unauthorized account of the early years at Disney's /
by Jack Kinney ; introduction by Leonard Maltin.
   p. cm.
   1. Kinney, Jack.   2. Animators—United States—
Biography.   3. Walt Disney Productions.   I. Title.
NC1766.U52D544   1988
741.5′8′0979493—dc19   88-18063
                                            CIP

ISBN 0-517-57057-2
10 9 8 7 6 5 4 3 2 1
First Edition

Contents

Acknowledgments 6

Foreword 7

Preface 9

Chapter 1: Off the Street, into the Trenches 11

Chapter 2: Life Among the Inmates 27

Chapter 3: The Story Department 59

Chapter 4: More Story Stories 77

Chapter 5: Sports 95

Chapter 6: On to Features 107

Chapter 7: Back to Shorts 121

Chapter 8: The Frenetic Forties 131

Chapter 9: Walt 147

Chapter 10: The Evils of Drink 159

Chapter 11: Latter Days 171

Epilogue 198

About the Author 199

Notes on the Characters 200

Acknowledgments

My gratitude to the three *J*s who contributed so much:
Jane Kinney
Jack Cutting
Joe Grant

To Melissa Schwarz and Don McKenzie: thank you both for transforming my memories, from storyboards to published books.

And for hours of speedy computer Wordstarring, my thanks to Darline "Busy Fingers" Henely.

Foreword

Jack Kinney was a hero of mine long before I ever knew his name.

Let me explain: In 1964 I made the first of many visits to the New York World's Fair in Flushing Meadows, New York. It was a wonderful place for a kid, full of fascinating exhibits and rides, and exotic foods like the newly imported Belgian waffle. But the dominant figure at the Fair was Walt Disney, whose team of imagineers had conceived and executed most of the best attractions on the premises.

The Disney "exhibit" that I visited most often, however, was the least publicized at the Fair. It consisted of a pair of modern-looking shells that housed movie projection units; they were placed along the perimeter of the IBM pavilion and featured old Disney cartoons on a continuous loop. The idea was to keep people entertained while they were waiting on line. For some reason, both shells featured Goofy cartoons: *Hockey Homicide* and *Hold That Pose*. I fell in love with both of them, and every time I returned to the Fair I'd run to the line outside IBM and watch them both, at least once. *Hold That Pose* features Goofy as an amateur photographer and contains one of my all-time favorite sight gags: The hapless shutterbug winds his film to the first exposure and looks through the little window in his camera to see the number 1; before that number finally appears, a series of dots perform a virtual ballet, and even turn into an old-time player piano roll! *Hockey Homicide* is one of the great Goofy sports cartoons, with some of the most violent and frenetic gags ever cooked up for that series; I particularly recall the two combative players (both portrayed by Goofy) who spend the entire game clobbering each other and being sent to the penalty box.

To be sure, one doesn't see these cartoons mentioned alongside *The Three Little Pigs* or *The Old Mill* as milestones in Walt Disney's career. But I'll match them, laugh for laugh, against the *funniest* cartoons ever made at the studio. And they were both directed by Jack Kinney.

Later, when I began to study the history of animation, I learned that Jack Kinney had been responsible for *many* of my favorite Disney cartoons (like *Der Fuhrer's Face*), not to mention some of the best sequences in the Disney features (like the Pink Elephants' nightmare in *Dumbo*).

Finally, more than twenty years after my Goofy cartoon binge at the World's Fair, I got to meet Jack Kinney and tell him how much I enjoyed his work. He in turn showed me a manuscript he'd been working on, recounting his colorful career at Disney's. I tried to thumb through it quickly, but I couldn't; once I started a passage I had to finish it, because practically every chapter had an anecdote or a gag with a punchline. I had a feeling, for the first time, what it was like to work at the Disney Studio.

Yes, there have been other books that traced the studio history; I wrote two of them myself. And there have been other first-person accounts—good ones, too. Still, I never had a sense of the day-to-day reality of life at Disney's until I read Jack Kinney's manuscript. He gave me a sense of the mundane as well as the magical—what it was like to start at the bottom, how far a paycheck really went in the depths of the Depression, what it was like to play softball with the boss, how Roy Williams earned his reputation as the funniest guy on the lot, and so much more, including memories of the bitter Disney Studio strike in 1941.

Best of all, these vignettes were all accompanied by Jack's lively and expressive drawings—the same kind of drawings, I imagine, that were tacked on bulletin boards, and taped to office doors back in the 1930s and 1940s, when (I gather) animators spent at least as much time producing gag cartoons for each other's benefit as they did for the films they were supposed to be working on.

Now that manuscript is a book, and everyone who cares about animation history can share Jack Kinney's memories, observations, and infectious sense of humor.

I only wish every copy of the book could be accompanied by a copy of *Hockey Homicide* or *Hold That Pose,* so all of you could be introduced to Jack Kinney's work the way I was. But I guess I shouldn't worry; there's hardly a person alive who hasn't been entertained by the cartoons he helped to create. And now we can go behind the scenes and learn what it was like when those precious and timeless films were made.

LEONARD MALTIN

Preface

For many years, the general moviegoing public was under the impression that Walt Disney did all the work on his pictures. Unlike the other animation studios, Disney films carried no screen credits.

Actually, animation is a group effort, with many people contributing story, gags, direction, layout, background, sound effects, voices, and more. At Disney's, Walt functioned as the producer, idea man, and general pusher. His energy and taste kept everything moving.

Some truly believed that Walt was a godlike icon, a man who could do no wrong. They admired him, idolized him as a father image, and forgave his moods. Then there were those who saw him in a different light and never got too close to him. They recognized his large ego, manifested in a drive that kept him pushing himself to the limit, expecting everyone else to extend themselves, too. If not, bye-bye, there were too many others looking for jobs. "Fish or cut bait" was required, nay, insisted upon.

Even the guys who hated Walt's guts admired him for raising animation from a crude craft to an art form.

Whenever a bunch of us boys in the animation game get together, conversation invariably drifts to the "good old days." Someone always says, "Why doesn't somebody put this stuff down on paper?" There is always unanimous agreement, and everyone rushes off until the next time when, once more, all agree that something should be done to preserve the stories, tales, and memories so dear to our hearts—sentimental slobs that we are. I decided to do the story the night Roy Williams's waterfall burned down . . . but I'll save that tale for last. Suffice it to say that a lot of crazy and wonderful things have happened to us.

These are my personal recollections of the Disney Studio where I worked for more than a quarter-century. It is the story of the little people, the strivers, the doers. It is about the pranks, the gags, the human foibles we remember so lovingly, and about the growing pains suffered by all of us involved. The Golden Age of Animation was a glorious experience.

CHAPTER 1

Off the Street, into the Trenches

I t all started in February 1931. Dean and Glen Olson and I had just been "circulated" from the *Los Angeles Herald Examiner*. I was hired there as a bill collector (probably because I'm quite a big guy), but I'd been trying to get into the Art Department. That's what you had to do in those days. There was a Depression on. Jobs were scarce, period. But jobs for artists were the scarcest of all. Now Dean and Glen planned to buy a secondhand pickup and go around to the local farmers and collect eggs. I had an appointment with a man named Walt Disney out on Hyperion, but Dean and Glen said I could go in with them for a twenty-five-dollar investment if the job fell through.

Two days later, at 8:00 A.M., I arrived at Disney Studios, 2719 Hyperion Avenue, East Hollywood. There were four of us in the reception room: Frank Powers, Don Smith, Ralph Wolf, and I, all aspiring artists.

I had brought my sketches along—some caricatures, watercolors, a lot of action drawings—rough sketches, whatever was at hand. My mother was a very good artist, and she'd given me a lot of tips.

Caroline Shafer, Walt's secretary, said, "Walt will see you soon. . . ."

When I met Walt Disney, he said, "The job pays twenty dollars a week. Not good. Not bad. I can give you a job for twenty dollars a week, but it's liable to be only temporary, not steady."

"I'll take it," I said.

"Tell the girl out there to give you a Scripto and some hard leads. Then go in and sit with Frenchy. He'll show you what to do."

I got a contract, too! Nine pages long. I'd never seen anything like it.

(Economically, I would have been wiser had I accepted Dean and Glen Olson's generous offer. They both became millionaires. A third of Olson Brothers Egg Farms for twenty-five bucks! Oh well.)

was introduced to a tall, lean, long-haired, large-nosed, ascetic-looking French Canadian. His name was Gilles Armand René de Tremaudan, or "just call me Frenchy." He patiently explained my job: "Take this piece of paper, put it over these pegs, and make a drawing between these other two drawings. It's what's called an inbetween. The other two drawings are extremes. You are an inbetweener. I am an animator, and don't you forget it! Sixteen drawings, or frames, make a foot. Start in."

I was shown how to flip the drawings to check the path of action. Each drawing had to be in perfect alignment with the others or you'd get a jump in the film that you could see. Simple? No! It was tough at first, because every line had to be exact.

Then, of course, there was *speed*! Speed was essential. You couldn't fall in love with each drawing, because it would only be on the screen for a fraction of a second. It was the overall result that counted. Each scene was only a part of the picture. And in six and a half minutes, each picture

PENCIL MILEAGE

had to tell a story—with gags, lines of dialogue, special effects like wind, rain, or snow—all in tempo.

The picture we were working on was called *The China Plate* (1931). It was one of the Silly Symphonies—in black and white, of course—a glorious musical with dragons, villains, and a love story. The whole thing was depicted on an ornate china plate. As with most of the early Silly Symphony pictures, the tiny characters came alive as the camera moved in on them. It had plenty of special effects, too. These scenes were animated by Joe D'Igalo, a meticulous artist, who specialized in the really tough effects scenes. He was the first fine draftsman I'd ever met.

The Disney studio on Hyperion had been an organ factory before Walt remodeled it by tacking up fiberboard walls. The place was cut up into cells, with the tops left open, and only one door to go in and out. But some of the best animators in the field were working in those cells when I started, people like Les Clark, who eventually became one of Walt's "nine old men"; Norman "Fergy" Ferguson, a top-level animator responsible for many innovations in the field; Dave Hand and Ben Sharpsteen, who both directed and produced features later on; Jack King, who left Disney's for a while, only to return to direct a whole slew of Donald Duck pictures; Fred Moore, an immense natural talent who redesigned Mickey Mouse and gave him a real personality; and Roy Williams, great story and gag man, head Mouseketeer, and my old buddy from Los Angeles Fremont High School.

Bert Gillett and Wilfred "Jaxon" Jackson were the two directors at that time. Jaxon had just moved from animation into direction, while Gillett was the senior, having learned his craft back East. They worked closely with the three excellent studio musicians—Carl Stalling, Bert Lewis, and Frank Churchill.

The girls in the Ink and Paint Department, later known as "the Nunnery," were responsible for tracing the animators' drawings onto sheets of transparent plastic called cels, which were used for the final film. Hazel and Lily Bounds, sisters, were there when I started, as was Marcellite Garner, the voice of Minnie Mouse. Lily later became Mrs. Walt Disney.

Emil Flohri and Carlos Manriquez were the Background Department. Emil was the art editor of *Life* magazine at one time. Carlos played handball, so one of his arms was larger than the other.

ııııııııııııııııııııııı

Tucked away in a corner were Bill Garity, Bob Cook, and Jim Lowerre, who made up the technical staff, and someplace else was Mister Rogers, who handled all the studio maintenance.

Everybody was called by his first name except Mister Rogers, who carried this honor as the eldest statesman.

Sitting over a hot lightboard eight hours a day was hard on the athletes among us.

When noon came, we all pulled out our brown bags, ate swiftly, and adjourned to the vacant lot across the street for our daily softball game. Left field was on the side of a hill, center field was less hilly, and right field was flat, but covered with knee-high weeds. The infield was in a hollow filled with debris: tin cans, broken bottles, paper, pieces of wood—and gopher holes. All of this contributed to the fierce competition between the two studio teams—the Marrieds and the Singles.

Each game was hotly contested, with much yelling, kidding, griping, cheating, in an anything-to-win spirit, with a lot of laughs, which allowed all of us to forget our frustrations and the tough scenes lying back on our desks.

Walt was athletically uncoordinated, but what a competitor! Coming to bat one time, he hit a scratch grounder to second base; the second baseman, a good athlete, kicked away an easy out, letting the ball get past him into center field. The center fielder charged in to make the stop, but lo and behold, he inadvertently booted the ball into right field, leaving the right fielder no choice but to pick it up (it had stopped rolling) and make a spectacular throw to the third baseman, who tossed the ball to the second baseman, who dropped the throw.

In the meantime, Walt was starting his run to first base, but first he had to trip over the bat. By this time the ball had finally been relayed to the hapless first baseman. He juggled it as long as possible, then, just as he had possession of the ball, guess who arrived at first base? Walt, who bumped heavily into the poor guy and took another spill. As he was dusting himself off, the umpire declared him safe at first.

Lighting a cigarette, Walt turned to the first baseman and said, "Better watch the rough stuff, George, you're liable to hurt somebody."

Luckily I happened to be playing deep (or high) in left field at the time, so I had no part in the thrilling play, although I did have a good vantage point on the field from which to view this spectacular team work. One thing was for sure: No one, not anybody, was gonna take responsibility for throwing Walt out. Jobs were too scarce. And anyway, we didn't want to hurt his ego.

We were all just a crazy bunch of young guys. Even Walt was only thirty at the time. But he was sort of a father figure to us. He paid the salaries, and that was damned important in the Depression.

Rumor has it that when Walt was producing the Oswald the Lucky Rabbit pictures, before Mickey Mouse, there was a fair amount of apprehension among the staff as to whether they would be paid each week. If Walt's car didn't show up on Monday, they knew he'd had to borrow on it again. Maybe the money from Universal hadn't come in on time. He was working that thin. Still, he never missed a payroll.

Things had improved by 1931. Mickey was a huge success, and the future looked bright.

My first three months passed quickly. It was the end of the "nervous period." Would I get a raise, or . . . ? I got it! From twenty dollars to $22.50 a week. A letter confirmed the raise, thank goodness. Another three months—twenty-five dollars. I was learning my craft.

In three more months, $27.50. I was on my way, doing small scenes and pieces of scenes, learning how to animate. Twenty-seven-fifty! Ah, now I could afford a few more cans of two-bit beer at Charlie Rivers's.

Former bootlegger Charlie Rivers was truly one of the unsung heroes of the Prohibition era. He always had a sympathetic ear and did his best to ease us through our growing pains and counsel us on our "careers" in the animation business. Every few months the cops would raid Charlie's informal drinking establishment, and he'd have to move. We followed him for two or three years, remaining loyal customers until Prohibition was repealed.

Some nights we went down to ex-boxer Bert Colima's Taxi Dance Salon at Fourth and Main Streets, where ballroom dancing was taught for ten cents a lesson. Each "lesson" only lasted a chorus or two, then they'd stop the music and you'd have to give the girl another ticket if you wanted to keep on dancing. It was a rip-off, but it was fun.

I n 1931, the new neo-Spanish, two-story addition to the studio was completed and the Animation and Story departments moved into plush new quarters, with new desks, drapes, spittoons, chairs, even windows to look out of. Things were looking up.

A huge neon sign was displayed on the roof: MICKEY MOUSE STUDIO! People started tossing their unwanted cats over the wall, figuring a mouse studio would probably welcome the little darlings. Naturally, the girls in Ink and Paint did. They fed them and played with them, and then, one day . . .

One afternoon a short time after we moved in, we were told to report to the new sound stage, where we gathered promptly at five, all the boys and girls wondering what was up. What was up, was down! Gunther "Gunny" Lessing, who had just returned from a trip to New York, was introduced by Walt as the principal speaker. Gunny was the Disney attorney, the type of guy who could rattle off one of those monstrous contracts I had signed without blinking an eye. He came on strong with a terribly sad story of conditions in New York—people going around with the seats of their pants worn out, and other distressing news of the Great Depression—ending up by passionately asking us to take a 15-percent cut in salary. Fifteen percent of $27.50, by my rapid calculations, amounted to $4.12, or a net salary of $23.38 per week. If I'd had a beer, I would have been crying in it. But at least we still had our jobs and didn't have to join all those other people with their pants worn out.

When you're young and ambitious and healthy, you bounce back from adversity. The beer was curtailed. We all felt that by taking a 15-percent cut, we had helped the studio survive a desperate period. We went back to work harder than ever. Color was just coming in, and Walt, naturally, was the first to adapt it to the cartoon medium.

CHAPTER 2

Life Among
the Inmates

W alt's first attempt at using color was a Silly Symphonies picture titled *Flowers and Trees* (1932). It won him his first Academy Award and was really the beginning of his worldwide reputation as the man at the top in animation. But we inmates took it in stride, just hoping our luck would hold out and we'd keep getting paid. Some contracts were canceled, but a few raises were handed out. I was Ben Sharpsteen's assistant by then, and he was one of the best. My salary leaped to thirty-five dollars a week, but, more important, I had survived.

Walt was operating as the head coach by this time, and he had a crew of assistant coaches—Wilfred Jackson, Bert Gillett, Dave Hand, and Ben Sharpsteen. They kept the assembly line running, and run it did, as did the players, hoping to catch the eye of the head coach and gain a starting position on the team.

The roster was made up of a multifarious group of all ages, sizes, and origins, all fighting for gags, better and more animation, choice assignments, even fighting among themselves—all for a coach who liked to keep his team off balance. Walt was continuously moving players around to different positions, different rooms, changing, always changing, trying to find a winning combination.

About this time, the "unit system" was started as a way to train embryonic animators. The unit heads were like teachers, answering our questions and putting us back on track when we got stuck. I was assigned to Ben Sharpsteen's unit.

Ben had quite a collection of characters working for him. Besides Roy Williams and me, there were Jack Cutting (who later became a foreign diplomat when Disney's went worldwide), Cy Young (who later became head of Special Effects), Ugo D'Orsi (special-effects animator), and many others. We were housed in one large room. It was a motley crew, and Ben was a hard but fair taskmaster. He insisted on good draftsmanship, staging, and action analysis. You had to learn—no shortcuts, just do it right.

TWO TOUGH
BUT FAIR
GUYS...

BEN SHARPSTEEN AND DAVE HAND

Roy Williams and I had our little spats from time to time, but we were friends and we often traded rides to and from the studio. Roy owned a little Ford roadster, onto which he had welded a piece of railroad track to act as a "bumper." Roy was a stickler for safe driving. Occasionally he would use his bumper to point out a miscreant's poor "courtesy of the road" manners. At those times he became an avenging angel, running the offending car into the curb, sometimes severing a fender. He would then dismount from his vehicle and explain to the driver the error of his ways. A man of imposing physique and a commanding voice, Roy usually convinced them of their mistakes quickly. Then we would continue to our destination.

Riding with Roy, you never knew what would happen. You could end up in jail, or anywhere else for that matter. To quell his spirit, I tried to engage him in discussions of popular subjects like sports and sex. It wasn't always successful, however, for Roy was rather impetuous.

Roy and I were in and out of a lot of trouble over the years. He always referred to me as his "old Fremont pal" and "number-one friend," although the number-one rating was downgraded at times when we had our little arguments.

One such altercation started in Room 113 of the new building. There were nine of us in the room, and Roy and I sat back-to-back along the window. It was a Monday morning, so, as usual, all of us began to relate our weekend adventures.

Roy wasn't talking much, so naturally I started ribbing him. My back was toward him as I stood up to check a scene, and he was sitting at his desk, muttering, "Shut up, big-nose." Later I found out Roy's romance over the weekend hadn't gone too well, but not before I heard a loud squeak behind me (Roy always made chairs squeak). I turned just in time to see Roy launch a flying tackle in my direction. Next thing I knew, I felt my rear end go crashing through the glass of my drawing board. Finally we both slipped in the spilled cuspidor water, and that was the end of it. We had a lot of cleaning up to do—fast, before Ben came in. . . .

Times were tough, and sometimes you had to suffer to get what was coming to you. Ed Smith, another one of us who worked under Ben Sharpsteen, really did it the hard way. He was living on turnips and bruised fruit—and one day he passed out from malnutrition. He toppled right out of his chair, and Ben came in and found him on the floor. Later, Ben told Walt that he thought the guys going through the "tryout period" should get eighteen dollars a week. Then they could eat at a popular greasy spoon across the street, like everybody else. Walt agreed.

About this time, George Drake was put in charge of all the inbetweeners—about twenty or thirty new guys. George was an irascible sonofabitch with a terrible temper and a short fuse. He watched over the poor bastards in the Bull Pen through a glass window, and woe betide anyone who got the least bit out of line.

George's group serviced all of us budding animators by doing our rough inbetween pencil tests, and that was fine with us, because it meant that we could concentrate on our animation. The only fly in the ointment was George. He was frustrated, having been relegated to his position of power because he had flunked animation. He made it as tough on us as he possibly could. Naturally, we ignored the silly SOB.

One day, however, Roy Williams and I were having a particularly rough time with Ben, who was chewing us out about some of the finer points of animation in our scenes. George Drake, who was standing in the door at the time, overheard our distress. Shortly afterwards, while Ben was out of the room, George showed up and announced, for all to hear, that henceforth we were to do our own gawdamned inbetweens.

Now, Roy and I were both pretty good-sized guys; we had played football together at Fremont High, Roy as a tackle and me as an end. That was all we needed to take action. George was very goosy, this we knew, and without any prearranged signal, Roy and I shoved our thumbs up George's rear end and lifted him off the floor. We ran him down the hall, out the front door, down the walk, and through the front gate, and deposited him in the center of Hyperion Boulevard. All this time, he was screaming like a stuck pig, which, indeed, he was.

Roy and I returned to our rooms to a thunderous ovation. We went back to our drawing boards, our feelings mollified, and started making the changes in our scenes—only to be interrupted by Ben Sharpsteen. George had tattled. Ben admonished us slightly, then had George appear and announce that his department would continue doing our inbetweens.

Leo Durocher's pronouncement notwithstanding, good guys do sometimes win.

Another of Ben's boys who needed watching was George Lane—a six-foot-three-inch redheaded string bean. George was a classy dresser, in white flannel pants, sleeveless sweaters, Barrymore collars, and navy sportcoats with gold buttons. He had the longest feet of anyone in the studio and always wore black-and-white golf shoes, which accentuated their length all the more. Naturally, he drove a blue Ford roadster loaded with extras and cute dollies.

On Mondays, George took his R-and-R in the men's can, but he was easily spotted by Ben Sharpsteen, who often said, "If it moves, it's a stump; if not, it's George." Somehow, George had a penchant for doing the wrong things at the wrong times.

Ambrosia Paliwoda (we called him Ambi) had quite a temper and some pretty unusual habits, though he was a very good artist. He liked to pick up beat-up old Cadillacs—for twenty-five-dollars or so. When they broke down he'd just leave them. He must have left ten cars scattered around the streets.

One day he found Walt on the road with a flat tire and gave him a lift into work. From that day on Walt liked him just fine.

Ben watched out for his boys. Some of his boys took care of Ben, too, although not necessarily just the way he wanted. As the studio grew, company romances became quite common (we used to call it "dipping your pen in company ink"), and the shack-ups all signed Ben Sharpsteen's name in the motel registers. Ben was a real straight-arrow, no-nonsense kind of guy, but his name became the "John Smith" of the naughty boys in the Magic Kingdom.

Gags were the name of the game, and not just for Mickey, Pluto, and the Goof. We had the old Limburger-cheese-on-the-light-bulbs-under-an-animator's-desk trick, paper cups pinned to the backs of chairs so that when an animator leaned back, the water squirted down the back of his neck—it went on and on.

The victims of these so-called jokes always had a standard comeback: "Why in hell don't you guys put them funny gags in the pictures?"

Well, sometimes we did, and for extra money, too—as much as $3.50 for an accepted gag and as high as twenty dollars for a sequence. Extra-curricular gag meetings took place every time a new picture was put into production, or about once a week. At each meeting, outlines were handed out. For example:

There will be a gag meeting in the Sound Stage at 5:30 P.M., May 3, 1932. Hand in your gags from the last meeting. New story line—Shanghaied, with Mickey, Minnie, Peg Leg Pete, and misc. characters. What funny pieces of business can you come up with? Director: Gillett; Music: Churchill; Outline: Pete kidnaps Minnie and takes her aboard his pirate ship. Pluto awakens Mickey. They follow spoor to Pete's ship. Mickey sneaks aboard the vessel as it is about to go to sea in a huge storm. Pete has Minnie in his cabin and is trying to make love to her; Minnie screams; Mickey runs in and challenges Pete with a swordfish he has taken from the wall. They duel as Minnie, tied to chair (with wheels), slides back and forth as the ship pitches in the violent storm. Pete almost overcomes Mickey, but Mickey cleverly overcomes the villainous Pete. (Chance for good gags here.) Then Mickey has to fight the entire crew. Mickey triumphs, but Pete manages to escape, then trips over Mickey, falls overboard and is chased over the horizon by a group of hungry sharks. Mickey and Minnie kiss as we iris out. I think this picture has a good chance for funny gags so bring 'em in next week. Go to it, gang. WALT.

Any usable ideas were paid for in *cash* at the meeting. This was over and above salaries, and in those days every buck counted and was eagerly received. You could actually feel the loot, and that gave each of us a real psychological boost.

Bill Herwig, layout man and illustrator, had spent a considerable time in the South Pacific, where he accumulated some rather startling characteristics, including a vast, salty vocabulary.

As soon as he was hired, along with three others whom he promptly dubbed "the slaves," Bill set up living quarters in the room where they worked. His gear consisted of a battered bedroll, a batch of patched clothes (which he laundered in the men's can), a tattered blanket, and his pride and joy: a cast-iron hibachi stove, "souvenired" from an unwary China trader. With this Bill made himself at home, all snug alow and aloft.

A trip down to L.A.'s Chinatown and Bill was prepared to sustain life with Oriental cuisine beyond belief. One evening, after "the slaves" had departed, mysterious aromas drifted down the hall and struck the Kansas City nostrils of one of the company's officers as he returned from a late-night stint with his ledgers. Nose twitching like Pluto's on the scent of a fire hydrant, the officer soon discovered the source—Bill, crouching over his banzai brazier, crooning a Tahitian love song.

Sensing foreign-devil, round-eyes upon him, Bill scowled up at his visitor with a friendly grimace.

"Whoinhell are you? Want chow? Here, have some!"

His startled guest politely declined, mumbling something about having just had supper.

Regaining his sense of the fitness of things, the visitor gazed intently around the room and ventured, "Do you really . . . sleep here?"

"Sure, where else, pally?"

"And what does the company say about this? Do they know?"

Bill forebore to blast this nosey nincompoop and let him off with, "Does the goddam company know? I don't give a damn if they do or not!"

"Do you mean to say they don't pay you . . . enough?"

Bill gulped a snort from an evil-looking ceramic jug and bellowed, "Enough? hoo hoo! I could make more pullin' a ricksha!"

Thinking it wise to placate this madman until other means could be devised for disposing of him, the visitor handed Bill his business card, saying, "If that's the case, why don't you come and see me in the morning?"

The next day the "slaves" came shambling in. Bill was up and hard at work, whether he was paid enough or not. The usual morning interrogation went into session. Bill grumbled that some company stooge had come snoopin' around, even left his card, no less.

All ears popped up. "Lessee it, Willie!" Bill groped in a shirt pocket and came out with a smeared bit of pasteboard. The inscription read:

Roy A. Disney
Vice President
Walt Disney Studios

When the initial shock died away, the "slaves" commiserated. "So long, Bill, you just did your hara-kiri act." "Naw, I bet you get something out of this." "Yeah. A trip down the sewer. Clean out your desk before you go. You are going, ain'tcha? Roy ain't a bad guy, by all accounts."

"Sure, I'm gonna see the sombitch. Got an engraved invitation, haven't I?" Bill stalked out the door and down the hall.

In Bill's absence his friends conjured up all sorts of ominous predictions, but these were shattered with a loud cough from the doorway. With an imperious gesture, Bill said, "He was like putty in my hands. The sombitch even gave me a raise . . . two and a half bucks a week!"

O f all the great animators spawned by the Disney animation factory, Norm Ferguson was one of the most overlooked. Fergy started in the business as a bookkeeper for Pat Sullivan (Felix the Cat) in New York, but because he was in accounting, he knew what the animators were making—a lot more than he was. So Fergy decided to become an animator, and in no time at all he became one of the best. Fergy was one of Walt's first recruits, after Ub Iwerks, Ham Hamilton, Rudy Ising, and Hugh Harman left to strike out on their own in the late twenties. In on the same wave came Jack King, Bert Gillett, Tom Palmer, Ben Sharpsteen, Dave Hand, and Harry Reeves. They had all been working in New York and had a lot of experience, some going back as far as the pioneer, Winsor McCay.

They were all good, but Fergy was outstanding. He brought the characters to life. They breathed, they had weight, thoughts, real movement—and they were funny. Fergy introduced a new style of animation. Instead of finishing each drawing to perfection, he worked rough and straight ahead. This was unheard of at Disney's at that time. Everyone worked from one extreme to the next, cleaning up, ready for ink and paint if the scene was okayed. (Of course, that was a big *if*. Most scenes weren't perfect and many had to be done all over again.) But Fergy didn't stop to clean up, he just kept right on going—and he was fast. He couldn't wait to see what the action would look like. A lot of time and money had been wasted until then by cleaning up scenes that didn't work. Of course, the early animation studios hardly cared whether the action worked or not. If it moved it stayed in the picture, and nobody saw their scenes play until they were up on the screen.

But at Disney's, every scene was pencil-tested on negative film and then "sweatboxed" for criticism, before the drawings were finalized. Fergy really started this rough-test era. When Fergy animated, he did whatever was needed for the action. He didn't go to art school, so he didn't know that you couldn't make Pluto's eyebrows go up past the top of his head. He exaggerated everything, and that gave his drawings more life. Soon, everybody started drawing looser, and thinking more about the action than about how clean the drawings were or how tight the inbetweens were.

This opened up more freedom of movement as well as kept a scene from being overworked. It was a fresh approach that kept animators from going stale on their drawings.

Fergy was the first animator to animate a complete sequence in one scene! One hundred seventy-five feet without a single cut. It was sensational. Pluto stuck with flypaper while chasing a fly stands out in my mind as one of the finest and funniest pieces of animation I have ever seen, with Frank Churchill's music playing behind it. Part of a picture called *Playful Pluto,* it remains as fresh today as it was back in 1933.

This rough and loose style became the thing to do with all the young animators—especially when Walt liked it. Others, like Jack King, who were animating at the time, had been trained to draw with very clean lines and couldn't break the habit, no matter how hard they tried. Jack solved the problem by giving his scenes to his assistant, Roy Williams, to rough up before sending them to test camera.

The term *sweatbox* came into being during this early era in animation history and remains to this day. It can be used as a noun or as a verb, as in "my scene is being sweatboxed."

It all started with the moviola. A moviola was a miniature projection machine into which film was threaded and could be viewed on a small aperture in the machine itself. The projection speed was controlled by the operator. It could be stopped on an individual frame, or run back and forth indefinitely, depending on the stamina of the viewer's eyeballs. (Test scenes were shot in negative, resulting in white lines on a black background.)

In this way, scenes could be viewed by the animators to see if they were getting desired results. If any changes were required, it was back to the drawing boards for tinkering until the scene was ready to be presented to the director's critical eye. Then a group session was held "in sweatbox" over the steaming moviola. That's where the sweat came in . . . or rolled out.

In the early days of the studio, moviolas had to be leased by the manufacturer, and for a pretty penny. Consequently, there were only two available at the studio, and these were placed in small alcoves, one on each floor. These early gadgets didn't have a takeup reel, and the film running through went right onto the floor (they never seemed to hit the baskets provided), or, in the case of a long scene that had been patched into a loop, an assistant stood down the hall, holding the free end of the loop and passing it by hand to the machine. These moviolas also made a helluva racket in the confined space, and I recall one tyro asking who in hell was frying all that bacon down the hall—he couldn't smell it, but he could hear it.

A sweatbox session could determine a man's fate in the organization; a good session could lead to fame and fortune, a bad one to the other side of the main gate. Consequently, as the session progressed, the air became hot, then steamy, and even gamy as a result of all the perspiration, carbon monoxide, and shattered hopes floating about in the gloom.

In later years, when the studio became more affluent, the screening rooms became posh mini-theaters, complete with air conditioning, adjustable cushioned divans, and, for once, enough ashtrays for the nervous

butt-gobblers. But the basic function remained the same. The projection machine still inexorably ran backward or forward or freeze-framed right on target at critical fault frames, and the same doom-filled criticisms still rolled forth from the directors. Careers still shattered, air conditioning or no, and the same stunned victims still tottered out into the light, wondering how they ever could have animated so much disaster into one scene or one frame.

Someone once suggested that the new torture chambers should be renamed "perspiration parlors," but the name "sweatbox" stuck, and they are still called that. Now you can understand why.

When a picture was finished, it was usually previewed at the Alexander Theater in Glendale to get audience reaction. After the show, the boys and girls would gather in the lobby and discuss the various scenes along with Walt. One time Walt stood outside the theater and chewed out Rudy Zamora, a certain free-spirited animator. Walt dissected each scene in detail. Rudy (who hadn't even worked on the picture) waited until Walt was almost through, then asked:

"Hey, Walt, I only got one question."

"Yeah? What?"

"What makes them things move?"

There was a pause, then Walt said, "The assistant, while the animator sits on his ass!"

Walt always had a quick comeback.

Actually, Walt liked Rudy, even if he was a thorn in his side. Rudy was a top-notch animator and a very irreverent guy.

"BOY! ~ I WISH I COULD ANIMATE LIKE FRED...MAYBE...I'M USING THE WRONG KIND OF PENCIL!"

HERO WORSHIP

Freddie Moore was another animator who had a style all his own. He drew as easily as breathing, and as the saying goes, "He could draw his ass," a very high compliment. Freddie started with the studio when he was very young and became an animator almost overnight. He was a natural talent.

The stuff flowed off his pencil as fast as writing, and he drew on everything—newspaper, scraps, napkins—and gave his drawings away. His ladies were especially popular. I saved a few.

Freddie did wonders for Mickey Mouse and many of the other Disney characters. He put real eyes on Mickey and loosened him up to beat the band. Before that, Mickey was a flat, cardboard character, with dots for eyes. Freddie gave him personality.

Freddie was a real little gentleman. He'd go out of his way to help anyone he could. He was a very coordinated guy, too. Fred and I were in the same unit for a long time. He was a joy to work with, and a joy just to be around. That's how we all felt about him.

Bert Gillett was a stocky, well-built guy with boundless energy. He was the first director at the studio. Of course there were only two at that time, he and Wilfred "Jaxon" Jackson. Both were excellent.

Bert worked with Frank Churchill and Jaxon worked with Paul Smith. All day long we heard the pounding of the pianos and the beat of metronomes coming from the music rooms.

Bert Gillett's room was especially noisy, as Bert acted out all the parts, beating on the tables, chairs, or the piano top and hitting the rhythm with a heavy foot. This was where the Mickey Mouse music originated. Bert was the first "tink-tink-tink" director. Every time Mickey took a step, there was a metallic "tink." Minnie, Mickey, and Pluto were especially "tink-tink." Peg Leg Pete was more "thunk-thunk," but that gave contrast. The "tink-tink" style was played on the xylophone or bells, while the "thunk-thunk" was created with heavy sound effects. Everything moved to a rhythm and, by God, the animator better follow that beat, or the whole thing would be out of sync. Gillett was very energetic and so were his Mickey Mouse pictures—loud and fast.

Jaxon, on the other hand, was the Silly Symphonies director. He had an entirely different style. He used more classical music, catching the unusual phrasing and accents. Jaxon directed *Flowers and Trees,* the first Disney picture to win an Academy Award.

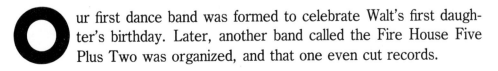

Our first dance band was formed to celebrate Walt's first daughter's birthday. Later, another band called the Fire House Five Plus Two was organized, and that one even cut records.

49

W alt's secretary, Carolyn Schaefer (otherwise known as Clara Cluck), loved company gossip and had a great knack for ferreting it out. She put together this first issue of the *Mickey Mouse Melodeon,* and it really caught on, coming out once a month for several years. Copies were made on the mimeograph and passed out to all Disney employees, who contributed bits and pieces as well. Later Carolyn married Frank Churchill, one of the great Disney musicians. She left the company, but I doubt she ever stopped clucking.

MICKEY MOUSE MELODEON

House Organ of the Disney Studio

Vol. 1   November 1932   No. 1

WE GO TO PRINT

This month marks the first appearance of our Studio paper. This is a pet idea of Walt's, which we hope to make into a monthly feature.

We are, as it were, giving you a sample ballot. It is up to you to write your own paper from now on. We will solicit news from all the gang. Please proof read all your own copy, because if Juanita does not get to it, I'll never recognize a misspelled word.

We ask your indulgence if any editorial weaknesses are detected—after all we are only wimmin and it has been a year or two since we edited the college weekly.

The Editor

DISNEY CARTOONS GIVEN PLACE IN ART EXHIBIT

The Philadelphia Art Alliance calling the Disney cartoons "A new type of American Art," has given the Mickey Mouse and Silly Symphony Cartoons a special exhibition in its galleries.

MICKEY MOUSE ELIGIBLE FOR SHORT SUBJECT AWARD

For the first time in the history of Academy awards, a special recognition is being made of the short subject this year.

Accordingly two of our subjects, "Mickey's Orphans" and "Flowers and Trees" were entered for consideration.

BASEBALL

Much to the sorrow of Johnny Cannon and Co., the Mickey Mouse Baseball team went down to an embarrassing defeat at the hands of Senor Carlos Manriquez and the Mexican Manglers—the toughest bunch of baseball bandits ever assembled outside of the Los Angeles R'lwy. The locals put up a strong battle throughout, but were heavily outnumbered by the Manglers and their two assistant umpires. Capt. Cannon promises a win for the next game as he will have his own umpire.

MUSIC NOTES

For the first time since the big Studio Shindig, our own Barnyard Band has finally got together and started on their Fall and Winter rehearsals this week.

Impossible Piano: "Drop Seat" Smith

Tramp Drummer:
"Hit Em Hard" Kinney

Bull Fiddle: "Silent" Sears

Screwey Sax: "Strip" Osborne

Terrible Tuba: "Signor Chukko" Coucho

Batty Banjo: "Hot Cha" Gray

Mussy Mandolin:
"Mister" (to you) Babbitt

Horrible Harmonica:
"Strawberry" Jackson

Slippery Trombone: "Loose Lip" Love

Cock-Eyed Clarinet:
"Pinto" (Whatta Tone) Colvig

CLARA CLUCK'S COLUMN

We hear our own Minnie Mouse has been seen places with a blond Apollo—hope it isn't serious—what would we do without our Minnie? . . . Bert Lewis has worn three different suits in the last week—is he giving in to his secret desires, or what?—one of them is the last word in hot-cha tweed . . . Ted Sears says when he is president he is going to order a special assortment of those little half-pint blonds—lots of guys would like to see Ted get the office . . . Burton Gillet has just moved into his new mansion—it has five bedrooms and five baths—each made in a different color harmony—Burton will have to wash his ears now—one of the baths is in that gorgeous warm red shade—looks like an ad for Standard Plumbing—Bert is all a-flutter—can't say we blame him . . . Frank Churchill was off the other afternoon to go to a funeral—we wonder why he went to the barber and got a complete working over first—it takes nothing short of a national calamity to make Frank go to the barber . . . If you want to see something funny, just drop in the gym at Hollywood High any Monday night and watch Emily Palmner, Juanita Lundy, and Frankie Luske cavorting around in the tap dancing class . . . Ed Love was seen going into an apartment with a certain Miss Fairborn the other night—he didn't come out until the morning——what's this Ed? . . . That's all folks see you soon again . . .

Lovingly,
Clara

51

Fred Moore and Fergy did all the animation on *Three Little Pigs* (1933), which was directed by Bert Gillett. Fred did the Three Pigs and Fergy drew the Big Bad Wolf. The picture was a sensation, and the song "Who's Afraid of the Big Bad Wolf?" won an Academy Award and became a national hit in the middle of the Depression. It was used by Roosevelt and political cartoonists as a symbol of hope in trying times. The lyrics were written by Ted Sears (head of the Story Department) and Pinto Colvig (the voice of Goofy), and the music was by Frank Churchill. The people *needed* a song like that. It really took off—and so did Bert Gillett, to New York and Van Buren Studios, who offered him quite a sum as the hit's director. He and Tom Palmer produced a new series there entitled *Molly Moo Cow* (a fiasco).

Bert's exodus really griped Walt, who said, "Who needs him, I'll direct in his place." And so he did, using his top animators from *Three Little Pigs*—Norm Ferguson and Freddie Moore. Walt moved into his own music room and started making *The Golden Touch* (1935), the King Midas story. This was a very hush-hush operation, with just two animators, who were sworn to secrecy. The entire studio awaited this epic, and finally it was finished and previewed at the Alexandra Theater in Glendale. All personnel turned out to see what Walt had wrought. He had wrought a bomb! *The Golden Touch* laid a great big golden egg. That picture was the last Walt ever directed. We knew better than to discuss it, ever. It was forgotten and the studio went on to other things.

Years later, Walt roared into Jaxon's office and started chewing him out about something or other. Jaxon was usually a very calm guy, but he was a redhead and this time he blew his cool. "Walt," he said, "I recollect that you once directed a picture called *The Golden Touch.*" There was instant silence. Walt stared at Jaxon, then stomped out, slamming the door.

As Jaxon described it, after a few beats the door opened and Walt's head popped back in. Wearing a heavy frown, and very slowly punctuating his words with his finger, he said, "Never, ever mention that picture again." Then he slammed the door and clumped down the hall.

Needless to say, it was never mentioned again.

By 1934 the studio had grown to more than two hundred people, and at last I became a full-fledged animator. I was assigned scenes all my own, and some sequences, in pictures like *Mickey's Steam Roller* (1934), *Two-Gun Mickey* (1934), *The Cookie Carnival* (1935), *Mickey's Fire Brigade* (1935), *Orphan's Picnic* (1936), *Mickey's Service Station* (1935), and *The Band Concert* (1935), the first Mickey in color.

The talent scouts continued to recruit more trainees as Disney animation developed at a furious rate. The results of the publicity were astounding. Thousands of applications came in. Sample drawings and portfolios were submitted and screened from all parts of the country as well as from many foreign lands. About fifteen hundred were chosen for further screening, and seventy-five who had outstanding talent were hired and given a tryout at the studio.

The new guys were a motley bunch, just like the inmates. They came from everywhere, in every shape and size. This gathering of types into the Disney melting pot gave the studio a fine cross-section of people with diverse backgrounds, habits, and religions, creating an exchange of ideas and drawing styles that added balance to the finished product.

Production continued, in spite of occasional mishaps. One time one of the new guys almost blew us all up! He was working as a gofer, running errands and delivering the rough-test film to the animators all day long.

This particular day he was just loaded with the stuff—it was all over his shoulders, around his neck, the whole bit. Nitrate film was highly flammable—explosive, really—but he hadn't been around long enough to realize how dangerous it was. Just a spark did it.

Anything was possible for the new animators the studio was training. Top teachers were hired and put on staff, such as Don Graham, Phil Dike, Rico LeBrun, and Bernard Garbutt. We had two or three night sessions a week, with live models. We studied life drawing, musculature composition, quick sketch, animals of all kinds, techniques, and action analysis.

The recruits from the New York studios represented the biggest new group. They tended to hang together at first, but soon they were assimilated—although there were some who really put down California. They missed the theater, opera, the Yankees, the Dodgers, and the excitement of New York.

Some of the guys from New York learned about sunshine, beaches, mountains, deserts, and lakes, as well as the casual dress of the native, and never went back. But Mike Balukas wasn't one of them.

Mike was a tall, handsome guy—well built, polite, a fine artist, and a real head-turner for the girls. He had everything, but he was a deaf mute. He could make certain noises, however, and could pantomime very well in order to make himself understood. He always carried a notebook in which he would quickly write out what he had to say or illustrate his ideas, if all else failed. He had a good sense of humor and did not let his affliction get in the way.

Everyone liked Mike, but that didn't stop them from pulling gags on him, just the same as everyone else.

It so happened that Mike was at Disney's when the Long Beach earthquake occurred, with its series of aftershocks. Since he was unable to hear, Mike set up a row of short pencil stubs on top of his desk, so that if there was a tremor, they would tumble down onto the drawing board. Thus alerted, he would scramble to safety—running down the hall, out of the building, and into Hyperion Avenue, yelling "ert-quake, ert-quake" in a high-pitched voice.

This paranoia was noted by several of the boys, of course. When things got a little slow they would sneak into the room next to Mike's and, all together, shake the wall, causing the pencil stubs to topple down. Thinking danger was imminent, Mike would zing away from his desk, out the door, down the hall, and out into the street.

Now, Mike was a fine athlete and could really make time reaching safety. So one enterprising animator with a stopwatch started timing Mike's exits and running book on bets with other gamblers.

Alas, after a while Mike Balukas had enough of crazy California with its earthquakes, and returned to New York, where a man could live safely.

The studio took advantage of the great diversity of talent they'd collected by asking for gags and story ideas from everyone. Even the gardeners submitted usable gags.

From my participation in gag meetings, I was given a tryout in the Story Department. I liked it very much. It was my cup of tea. Some of the best brains were in the Story Department, and I was invited to join this distinguished group.

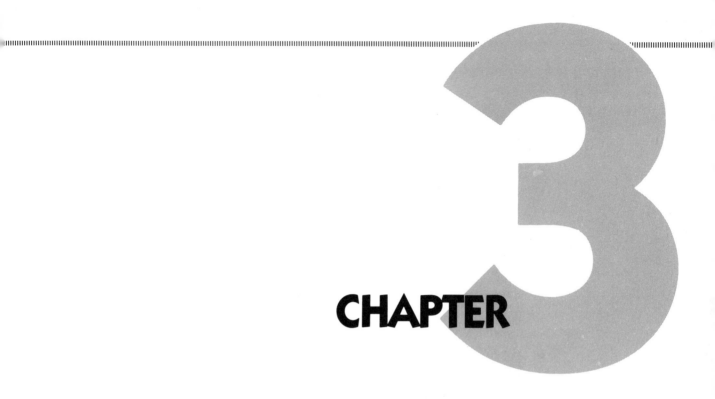

CHAPTER **3**

The Story
Department

When I got there, the Story Department was short-handed. Production was growing at such a rate that it was hard to keep up, and Ben Sharpsteen needed someone to supply his unit. This situation turned out to be my big break.

I had been so embroiled in the nuts and bolts of animation during my first few years with the studio that I didn't understand the most fundamental rules of the game. We animators took story for granted, feeling that our particular scenes or sequences were all that mattered. Not so. Our noses were too close to the drawing boards to realize that the material had to have its roots in an idea before it could be developed into the layout and exposure sheet phases from which we worked. How wrong our limited conception! Without a good story you've got nothing.

The studio was expanding so fast that Walt was forced to grab any space he could get. The Story Department was housed in a pair of old, weatherbeaten, termite-riddled apartment houses across the parking lot from the "classy" studio buildings. At least we had plenty of room. Most of us had separate offices, though we were constantly wandering from room to room, checking each other's boards.

Here are a few of the guys I worked with (from left): Carl Barks, Roy Williams, Webb Smith, Homer Brightman, Harry Reeves, Ted Sears, Otto Englander.

"HANGIN" OUT THE WASH

Each idea was kicked around among the peers, tightened up and adjusted until it had continuity. We'd start slowly, introducing the characters, sketching it out, and just keep milking the stuff until we were ready for a meeting with the director and Walt.

Before we had traffic boys, carrying your storyboards to and from meetings was part of being an "author."

Each guy had his own style for presenting. Some tried the "cool approach," acting a wee bit above it all, but that was really just a cover-up for incompetence. The best story guys could act up a storm, laugh uproariously at their favorite gags, and outshout everyone, while using a wooden pointer to emphasize the main elements.

Roy Williams added his own nuances with the "violent approach," kicking the boards and beating them to bits while he told the story. That was crazy to watch. He always had us in the palm of his hand, just like a used-car salesman.

Then there was the "emotional approach," typified by Homer Brightman. Homer was a real ham actor. One time he made a particularly dramatic exit with the line ". . . and the damned duck ran out to get away from the big ol' grizzly . . . quack, quack, quack." One of the boys got up and locked the door after him. We left him banging on the door and broke for lunch.

One of the New York contingent was an unforgettable character named Mike Myers. Mike was a typical "dese, dem, and dose" guy—a funny man and a darn good story and gag man.

Mike had been used as a floating gag man supplying all the units, but finally he was made a full-fledged story director, responsible for acting out his own storyboards.

About this time, Dave Hand was put in charge of developing stories for the shorts (Walt was pretty much tied up with feature productions). Dave was a very conscientious and meticulous boss. He tried to get all the bugs out before calling Walt in for his final okay, so everyone polished the gags and the business first to get Dave's approval.

It was Mike's debut in front of all the hard-nosed, experienced story guys. His story starred Donald Duck and Pluto. Mike took his position in front of the eight-by-four-foot storyboards filled with continuity drawings, and a hush fell over the assembled group.

Using Mike's vernacular . . .

"Well, we open on Donald Duck's house, it's early morning. The fuckin' sun's just peekin' over another fuckin' rooster, and boids start whistlin'. A cat yowls, Pluto wakes up an' starts chasin' the goddam cat, barking like a sonofabitch. All kinda noises are raisin' hell. Donald Duck leaps outta bed madder'n a goddam harnit. He trips over a pair of shoes and falls on his ass, then the fuckin' duck jumps to his feet an' runs out the fuckin' door. He sees Pluto chasin' that goddam cat up a nearby fuckin' tree, raisin' hell with that fuckin' cat. Then the fuckin' duck runs on, swingin' a rake at the goddam dog. As the fuckin' duck takes a big swing at ol' Pluto, his fuckin' unnerwear catches ta a clothesline hung with red unnerwear, a goddam nightshirt, anna lotta socks and other fuckin' stuff, the fuckin' duck gets hisself all fucked up with all the goddam clothes offa the fuckin' line an' he trips an' falls on his fuckin' ass again. . . ."

The guys are now laughing up a hurricane at Mike's recitation.

"Hold it!" yells Dave, over the uproar. "Hold it! Mike, hold it," he shouts.

Mike stops and says, "What the fuck for, I'm just gettin' started!"

"Yeah," says Dave, "but you can't tell a story like that!"

"Why the fuckin' hell not?" says Mike.

"You gotta clean up your dialogue," Dave answers. "Walt won't hold still for you referring to Donald as 'that fuckin' duck.'"

"Well, that's what he is, ain't he?"

"No!" roared Dave. "He's a duck . . . D-O-N-A-L-D D-U-C-K!"

"Have it your way," retorted Mike, "he's still a fuckin' duck and I don't care how you spell it!"

Then they both got real mad, and Mike said, "You can take that goddam fuckin' duck and stuff it up your ass! I'm goin' back to Noo Yawk where I can talk to somebody." Later, some of the guys got together and finished the story. It turned out to be a very cute picture.

Harry "Snackery" Reeves was a hard-nosed competitor and a typical Arrow collar man. He came from a poor family and, by golly, he wasn't going to be like that! Harry worked hard, played hard, and invested wisely. He was an inspiration.

When someone asks me, "How can I get a job in the animation business?" I think of Harry. It's got a lot to do with being at the right place at the right time. . . .

Harry Reeves, a budding young artist from Terre Haute, Indiana, went to New York to seek his fortune. He'd always wanted to work in the entertainment business, and his first step up the ladder was a motion picture theater (on Broadway!) that showed first-run movies. *Tarzan of the Apes* was playing, and as an added attraction the theater had on display in the lobby a real, live monkey. Well, somehow that monkey escaped and was soon cavorting atop the theater marquee. Harry was assigned to capture the creature, and he was in the middle of this rescue when Rudy Zamora, Charlie Byrnes, and Al Eugster happened to stroll by. They had stopped at the box office to inquire when the next animated cartoon would be shown, when they were interrupted by a voice from above.

"Hey, are you fellas in the cartoon game? I wanna be a cartoonist, too. How do I get a job?"

Looking up, they saw Harry and the monkey both chattering down at them. When Harry stopped for breath, they managed to tell him that indeed they were cartoonists, engaged by the Pat Sullivan Studio doing Felix the Cat, and at that Harry forgot all about the monkey.

"Where's the studio? Can I follow you fellas back? Maybe I can see Pat Sullivan an' getta job an' learn all about making them things move. I got a lotta ideas, an' maybe I can do gags! Let's go!"

Well, Harry kind of swept them off their feet. They took him back and introduced him to Pat Sullivan and he got a job. He started as an inker and painter, but with his enthusiasm, he soon got to be an inbetweener, and then became an assistant to Norm Ferguson, one of the top animators in the business. Fergy liked Harry and helped him learn the ropes. When Fergy got an offer from Walt (as did Rudy, Charlie, and Al), Harry went too, and soon they were all on the West Coast, working at the Mickey Mouse Studio. Harry became an animator, and then went into the Story Department and eventually became a director. But that's only half the story.

When he got to California, Harry opened a vegetable stand on Los Feliz Boulevard. He'd go to the wholesale market every morning at four o'clock, stock his bins with fresh vegetables, then go to work, where he had many steady customers.

When Prohibition was repealed, Harry took a freight car loaded with wines on consignment—and quickly sold all of it. Then he started dabbling in real estate, checking foreclosures and trading houses. He went into stamp collecting, invested in a liquor store, a dry-cleaning shop, gas stations, a café, insurance, and finally diamonds—you name it, Harry was in it. His drive was unlimited. And he always included us in his money-making schemes—all strictly legitimate. He hated to lose, though—whether it was matching pennies, football pools, card games, Monopoly, anything. Harry had dandruff, and, in times of aggravation, a habit of pulling at his shirt collar.

When Harry went to a college football game, he always stood in the high school kids' line, after parking a mile from the stadium to save money. Then he'd cheer for whichever team scored first, and as the tide turned, so would Harry's allegiance, changing teams as many as ten times during a game. Harry was one of a kind. He also became a millionaire.

SON-OF A BUCK

Ted Sears was the head of the Story Department. He was a fine writer with a tremendous sense of humor, and a soft-sell, easygoing type of guy. He was a New Yorker, always dressed well.

Ted could take anything you had and make it work; he'd nap through the noisiest story meetings and wake up with the perfect gag to solve any story problem.

Once, Ted and his wife were showing some New York friends around Knott's Berry Farm, a theme park in our area, before Disneyland. Someone suggested that it was time to have lunch, so naturally Ted, being a firm believer in a libation before eating, steered his guests toward the Western Saloon. But the so-called Western Saloon served nothing but fruit juices.

Ted was insulted and wanted to leave immediately, but his wife talked him out of it, and reluctantly he registered in the reservation book as "Mr. Byrdchitte and a party of four." The maître d' said it would be a short wait of twenty minutes and suggested they meander around the premises and enjoy the sights. Soon they were called over the loudspeaker—by their alias, which wasn't pronounced as it was spelled.

Another time, while looking up a number, Ted stumbled on a name that was just too good to pass up, and dialed it. The conversation went like this:

"Hello? Is this Gisella Werberserk Piffl?"

"Yes . . ."

"I'm an old friend of your brother's, we were classmates at Cornell."

"Oh, my brother didn't go to Cornell, he graduated from Princeton."

"I'm sorry, you must be some other Gisella Werberserk Piffl."

"A NAME DROPPER"

Everyone at the studio was asked to write up their opinion of the pictures, but Ted preferred to write them from Cy Young's point of view. Cy was a Chinese genius in effects animation, a painstaking job. Ted captured his speech perfectly.

This review was for *Song of the South,* a combination live-action/animated feature starring James Baskett from "Amos 'n' Andy," with Brer Fox and Brer Rabbit.

Brerrer Fox and his tar babies! Hot dog, ever since a small infant these half-wits have repulsed me with laughter to rolling in the aisles.

Ignorance portion of the audience will find trouble misunderstanding the dialect, but I'm greatest fan and pushover for darkey's talk (yay man).

When my imagination visulize those smoke effect—Swanny River with shimmer reflections and steam boats round the bend—I am forced to predicting greatest triumph of silver screens since Reluctant Dragon.

Cripes-all mighty. How it brings home to our mind the foolish prejudices between ignorant dam southerner and fine old Yankees people when Mr. Ream is shooting one arm off of snooper who hides in the tree branch with union suit. Whass it all goes to prove, I tell myself. And the answer is yes. Brotherly love is more powerful no matter which side of us is born above or below the Macy Dickeson line. Too bad all of this is so dam seldom; there for:

Who can help but for going wild with over-enthusiasm over reduced-budget feature production of Onku Ream Us. What an ambiguous tale of human interest! Full of effects animation, suspension and miscegenation, all these fine quality rolled inside one story yarn like fortune in rice cake.

Ted liked to tag people, too. Hugh Hennesy was "the assistant monk," Otto Englander "the hummingbird." Al Bertino (a very funny big brash Italian guy) he would call "the only man who could walk down the middle of the street in Tel Aviv and be shot at by both sides."

The unit managers were "straw bosses"—snooping and running back and forth to Walt with "interoffice communications." One night John Rose (a unit manager) came running up just as we were leaving five minutes early. Before he could say a word, Ted said, "Busy man, you've had a little day." It fit the guy perfectly.

On weekends, Walt would roam the premises and get a sneak preview of our storyboards. Then he'd come to the story meeting with a "fresh eye" on the material, and we'd all be amazed at his efficiency in juggling pieces around. We could always tell he'd paid us a visit if there were Chesterfield butts in the ashtrays on Monday morning.

Albert Hurter was one of a kind—a genius, really. A Swiss, he had studied under Heinrich Kley as a boy and was a very fine draftsman. He could draw anything; his imagination knew no bounds.

After emigrating to the United States, Albert became interested in the new medium of animation, and worked as an apprentice at the early studios in New York. He became a fine animator as well as a designer, model man, idea man, and layout and background man. He had an enormous reputation among the various denizens of our animation jungle, but not because he asked for it, as Albert was a very shy, private guy with his own wonderful sense of humor.

Albert arrived in the early 1930s, just in time for character development work on *Snow White* and many of the Silly Symphonies. His talents made a contribution to many of the best Disney pictures. He was often given free rein to pursue any direction he felt, and he felt plenty.

Albert always got to the studio at 6:30 A.M. to walk around the parking lot adjacent to our apartment houses, smoke his cigar, and read all the papers—until 8:00 A.M., when, well informed, he was ready to work.

Sometimes he was more informed than he realized. Ted Sears often brought him the papers, and Ted was an expert at meticulously doctoring the headlines to make them more sensational than intended. He'd take the most innocuous day and turn it into a disastrous one. Albert never discovered Ted's ploy, but he would always explode at the startling news: *"Mein Gott!* Vould you look vot dat crazy Hitler is doing now!"

Albert was a loner—he never married—and would work no other way. He insisted on living in an old hotel at Fourth and Main. There he could observe a great many offbeat characters and things, and his pencil would re-create them in far-out drawings of every kind imaginable.

At noon, Albert would emerge to walk around the studio, smoke his cigar, and stop to talk on any subject. As he walked, we noticed he had a tendency to limp slightly. One day I asked him about his feet. Did they hurt? Were his shoes too tight?

"Naw," said Albert, "my shoes, that's where I carry my cash. I do not trust some of the neighborhood people around Fourth and Main streets." Well, that was a simple answer from a complicated man.

Mary Flanigan was one of those rare individuals who never seemed to let anything bother her. She had a wonderful sense of humor and was always cheerful. That's a hard combination to beat! She was a short, roly-poly gal, and a born diplomat from Kentucky who spoke with a mixture of an Irish brogue and a deep Southern accent. If you can believe that.

Mary's real job was as a receptionist in the new Animation Building, but on the side she sold cigarettes for fifteen cents, cigars ranging from five to twenty-five cents, and peanuts or a hard-boiled egg for five cents. She also loaned money and carried people on the cuff until payday.

Mary's uncle happened to be Colonel Bradley, one of the best horse trainers in the land. From him, Mary learned the art of handicapping horses. Naturally, she used this lore to run her own booking agency as a service to some of the boys. It was a casual thing, but a nice service for those unable to visit the tracks during working hours.

Of course, out of all the characters at the studio, there were a few welshers—one was Earl Duvall, a charming story man who kept a tab running with Mary. Earl drove a snappy eight-cylinder Auburn runabout roadster. He dressed well, bought his clothes at elite men's stores, and ate lunch at Leslie's Bar and Hardware Store—the studio "in" place. In fact, Earl was the spitting image of the Prince of Wales at the time.

However, rumor had it that Earl lived beyond his means. He would sometimes go on the cuff for over a month, but somehow his horse would come in, and Mary always got paid first.

Now, Ted Sears's large corner office was a sort of gathering place for the department. Walt would drop in from time to time to see how things were going, and Earl, who was sort of a loner, would drop in too, to check on his horse bets for the day. Whenever he bumped into Walt, Walt would ask him how his story was going, and Earl would say, "Fine, just fine," which seemed to satisfy Walt.

After several weeks, Walt asked Earl when he would like to have a story meeting, and Earl answered, "I'm trying to tighten up the boards." "Well," Walt replied, "let me know when you're ready, and we'll get together." "Okay, Walt, it won't be long."

This went on for some time, and finally, one Friday, Walt said to Earl, "Let's set up a time and see what you've got." To which Earl said, "How about Monday at ten A.M.?"

That was fine with Walt, who told Ted to set up a meeting.

Monday morning arrived, as it usually did, and the troops assembled in Earl's room with Walt and four empty storyboards, but no Earl. We waited awhile, and still no Earl. Walt became impatient, tapping his fingers and wondering where Earl hid his boards. We searched around, but there were no clues, and no Earl either.

Earl had taken this time to terminate his employment with the Walt Disney Studios and had simply disappeared, leaving Walt holding the bag and also several bill collectors, including the Auburn car agency, who would have liked to repossess Earl's speedster. Another bag holder was Mary Flanigan, with a sizable chit for eggs, peanuts, and twenty-five-cent cigars. Mary wasn't worried. She knew Earl always paid.

About a week later, Mary received an envelope filled with cash, paying Earl's bill in full. Mary said, "See, you've got to trust people." Little did she know that Ted Sears and the boys had chipped in to uphold the honor of the Story Department.

4

More Story
Stories

Although the Story Department was out of the mainstream of production, our apartment houses had certain advantages. For one, they were situated on Griffith Park Drive, just a few blocks from John Marshall High School.

During football season, if we were ahead of schedule and waiting for a meeting, we could climb out the first-floor windows (thus avoiding the attendant at the studio gate) and go up the street to enjoy the games. Of course, we were too cheap to pay twenty-five cents for a ticket in the grandstands, and we soon discovered that by climbing up an ivy-covered bank we had a first-class, close-up view of the action on the field through a chain-link fence.

Well, for some reason the school principal took umbrage at our free-loading and made it a point to run around the end zone and tell us to come inside and pay. We refused, saying, "No, we're just fine where we are."

After several games he began to lose his temper, and one day he simply turned the sprinklers on under us. We slipped and slid down the ivy, and soon we were soaked to the skin. Taking the hint, we departed the premises, climbed back through our windows, and started to dry out.

Just when we returned, John Rose's secretary informed us that Walt was on his way over for a story meeting at 4:00 P.M. The warning gave us barely enough time to get rid of most of the mud, but we were still soaking wet when Walt made his appearance. We were a miserable bunch, but Walt pretended not to notice as he concentrated on the meeting.

Roy Williams could sit down and grunt out a few pounds of gags as if it were nothing.

For relaxation, we all would quick-sketch gags meant to be insulting, sarcastic, or even funny. This usually called for retaliation in a like manner. Woe betide the poor guy who had any outstanding facial or physical defect.

There was certainly no dearth of material to draw from. Fat, skinny, short, tall, bald, pimply, grumpy—whatever, they laid you out. My greatest "admirer" was Roy Williams, who himself was a big, fat, balding, hotheaded, unpredictable bastard. Roy called me "Banana nose," "Proboscis," "Anteater," and other endearing names. My brother Dick, who often worked with Roy, was simply called "Potato nose."

One of Roy's favorite gags about my nose was from high school days. He would say, "Oh yes, when Jack 'Ol' Banana' played football, our team always got a penalty. If Jack lined up as an end, there would be a quick whistle because his nose was offside. If he compensated and played off the line, there'd be another quick whistle and we'd lose another five yards for having five men in the backfield."

One Monday morning, Roy showed up at work in a god-awful mood, with his nose heavily bandaged and his eyes swollen. When I questioned him about his condition, he didn't answer, locked his door, and refused to open it for anyone.

Naturally, I was burning with curiosity. It wasn't like Roy to keep anything from me. I was his confidant on everything—sex, hangovers, gossip, sex, food, booze, sex, world events, sex, women, cars, finance, sex, politics, dames, gals, sex. Sometimes we would even discuss art. All these confidences I kept, which I reminded him throughout that long morning. All I got for my entreaties was, "Beat it, Big Nose."

Finally, around noon, Roy opened the door and told me what had happened. It seems that he and his date had decided to visit the Los Angeles Museum on Sunday—first, because it was free and he was broke; second, because it was a nice day; and third, because it was the perfect cultural pastime to while away the hours until nightfall. And then—romance!

Now, to understand the mechanics of this story, you must understand that Roy, a large man, was driving a small Plymouth convertible at that time.

Roy pulled into a parking place outside the museum and opened his own door, so that he could go around and gallantly open the door on his girl's side. But, for Roy to exit on his side, he first had to squeeze out from under the steering wheel, turn, move his rear bulk out the door, and follow it with the rest of his body. As he was performing these gymnastics, Roy was also doing what animators called an overlapping action. Reaching for the now-open door with his left hand, he backed from his car and swung the door closed as he pulled his head and shoulders in the general direction of out—when, blam! he caught his nose between the door and the top of the car. Luckily it was a soft top, but Roy did sustain a slightly broken nose.

From this time on, the nose gags became less prevalent.

Roy kept a carafe of drinking water on his desk and was known to toss it at the source of disagreements. My brother Dick always protected himself with a loaded water pistol, which, with deadly aim, he could use in retaliation.

Because of his overhanging physique, Roy never noticed, resulting in much amused speculation about his bladder capacity.

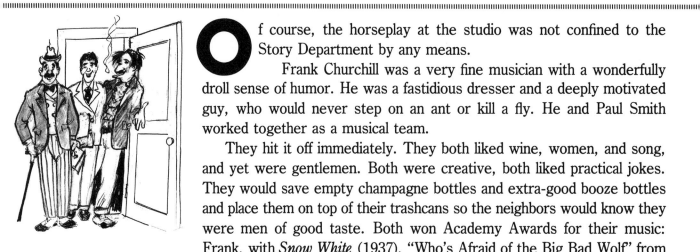

Of course, the horseplay at the studio was not confined to the Story Department by any means.

Frank Churchill was a very fine musician with a wonderfully droll sense of humor. He was a fastidious dresser and a deeply motivated guy, who would never step on an ant or kill a fly. He and Paul Smith worked together as a musical team.

They hit it off immediately. They both liked wine, women, and song, and yet were gentlemen. Both were creative, both liked practical jokes. They would save empty champagne bottles and extra-good booze bottles and place them on top of their trashcans so the neighbors would know they were men of good taste. Both won Academy Awards for their music: Frank, with *Snow White* (1937), "Who's Afraid of the Big Bad Wolf" from *Three Little Pigs,* and *Bambi* (1942); and Paul for various Silly Symphonies and the True Life Adventure series.

Frank wrote foot-tappin' and whistlin' music. Paul leaned more toward the classics. Both could play the piano like crazy and were always available for jam sessions. I admired and respected both, and enjoyed drinking with them as well.

Now, Walt didn't really understand musicians. He had a tin ear and couldn't keep a beat, but he knew the right result when he heard it in the pictures. He left Frank and Paul pretty much to their own devices . . . of which they had plenty.

One day, after lunch, Walt was showing off his studio to Charlie Chaplin and H. G. Wells. He had just walked them upstairs from the Animation Department toward the Music Department, busily explaining the various functions of the studio. Just as he opened the door he said, "And here's the room where the boys are composing the music for *Snow White.*" The two distinguished guests peered past Walt, and this is what they saw. . . .

Indeed, Walt's habit of dropping in unexpectedly was well known to all. One day he dropped in on Dick Huemer, another great story man who worked with Joe Grant as a team. Dick was in the process of shaving with his new electric razor. Hearing the familiar cough at the door, Dick's reflexes told him he'd better look busy, so he quickly shoved the razor into his pocket. Unfortunately, he neglected to shut it off.

"What the hell," said Walt, as Dick sheepishly pulled out the razor. "How do those things work?"

"Fine, jus' fine," answered Dick.

"Lemme try it," said Walt. And he did, saying, "I got to get me one of those." Then they got into production talk.

85

Earl Hurd and I shared a room for a time. Earl was one of the pioneers, and a very eccentric man. He invented cels, and a lot of
other devices that revolutionized the animation business.

Earl was a dapper guy, New York–style. He wore a pinstriped three-
piece suit, silk shirts and ties, a fedora, a paisley scarf, gray spats, a
camel's-hair polo coat, and gloves, and he sported a long cigarette
holder—an ideal outfit for the cold Eastern climate. But Earl wore this
ensemble in the hot California weather, too. I really didn't agree when he
insisted on keeping the windows closed and the drapes drawn to keep out
a vagrant breeze. I'd complain about our working conditions, and he'd
counter that he was just trying to acclimatize to our weather.

One day when Earl was out attending a story meeting, I decided *I*
wanted to acclimatize to the weather, too. I removed the three windows

and hid them, pulling the drapes over the holes. Earl didn't notice they were missing for several weeks.

Then one day there was a car crash in the parking lot, and when Earl pulled back the drapes to investigate, he discovered the windows were gone. Instant sneezing and chills shook his frame. He lost his temper and stalked down the hall, accusing those damn gag men of playing a dastardly joke.

As soon as he left, I quickly replaced the windows.

When he returned, I pulled the curtains wide, telling him that perhaps somebody had just washed the windows and he hadn't looked closely enough. Earl agreed that he might have been a little hasty and apologized to all.

Earl loved chickens. He had a pet chicken, too, named Biddy. He'd bring her to the studio, where he made a nest for her on his desk. He was doing a story with Pluto and chickens, titled *Mother Pluto* (1936), and he claimed he used her for research.

Earl was forever tinkering. He had a complete workshop set up in a spare bedroom, with a lathe, a bandsaw, a sander, and welding equipment. When he started up his various tools, it shook the whole house. His long-suffering wife, Svea, put up with it, however, not even minding his penchant for table lamps that, when turned on, depicted waterfalls and forest fires. He had at least a dozen of these strewn around his front room, a very scenic sight.

Earl invented a great number of labor-saving devices, such as an attachment for opening and closing his wrought-iron gate to save having to get out of his car. It worked well until rain flooded it, leaving the gate opening and closing like a swinging door.

Another one of Earl's inventions was more successful. This was a system that lifted his chickens in a suspended cage, rolled newspaper underneath to collect the droppings, and scraped them off into a container where they were saved for fertilizer. Ingenious!

Cy Young once rented a guest house from Earl, but had to move because Earl would fire up his machinery if he had a new idea at any time during the night. Cy claimed it interrupted his sleep.

Visits from the main studio were rare, but during the development of *Fantasia* (1940), space was at a premium, and a few intrepid souls discovered that behind our apartment houses was a fenced-in backyard, overgrown with weeds and debris. This haven promised a perfect setting for staging and photographing live-action routines for the "Dance of the Hours" sequence.

One day, there they were on our premises. One of the secretaries, who had taken ballet lessons, was dressed in a lovely pink ballet costume, rehearsing to a portable, hand-wound phonograph playing a classical recording of Debussy's lovely theme, recorded by the Philadelphia Symphony Orchestra, conducted by Leopold Stokowski.

From the weeds and debris of the sylvan glade, the melodic strains wafted through our open windows, quickly drawing the Story Department's curious inmates, who didn't mind offering suggestions to the perspiring artistic dance director. Ignoring us, she bravely continued her terpsichorean research until the sun set, when the valiant troupe packed and departed, as did the story crews.

I'm sure the research proved to be of immense value to the animators in creating the fine, finished animation that became a highlight of *Fantasia.*

Once, Walt was approached by KFI radio in Los Angeles, to do a show using all of his characters. Some of the voices were already set—Pinto Colvig, ex-actor, clarinetist, and now the voice of Goofy and Pluto; Clarence Nash, the one and only voice of Donald Duck; Marcellite Garner, a former inker and now the voice of Minnie Mouse; little Billy Bletcher, former Keystone Kop, and now the voice of Peg Leg Pete; and of course Walt, doing Mickey. But auditions were being held for other character voices. Stuart Buchanan, the talent scout, was in charge, and he set up in the apartment house with the Story Department.

One hot, quiet night, for want of something better to do, we started a rumor, with Homer Brightman once again as the patsy. We told him that Walt wasn't going to have time to do Mickey on the radio and was looking for a substitute. Homer fell for it and went around the next day practicing in a high falsetto: "Hello, Minnie. Hi, Pluto, heh, heh, heh . . ."

We convinced Homer he was a natural and set up an audition starting at 7:30 P.M. The mike was turned on and the audition began—with the entire Story Department hiding out upstairs in the next building, catching the act through the windows.

Stuart was in the booth. After each reading he would emerge and offer suggestions: "That was fine, Homer, but we need more action in the reading, so could you hop up and down when you read the lines? Okay, take twenty-three."

Homer hopped.

"Homer, you're out of mike range, would you hold the mike as you jump? Okay, take thirty-seven."

By ten o'clock quitting time, Homer was exhausted, sweating and pooped, but still game. Hop, hop, hop. "Hello, Minnie. Hi, Pluto, heh, heh, heh!"

"Hold it, Homer," said Stuart. "Now your socks squeak. We'll try it again when we have more time."

W alt liked to contribute in story meetings. He was a very good editor and could spot story weaknesses like no one else. Also, he had an advantage, in that we were usually too close to the stuff on the storyboards.

Most meetings were recorded by a stenographer, especially if Walt was in attendance.

Here's the transcript of part of a story meeting for one of my Goofy pictures.

TIGER HUNT [Released as Tiger Trouble, 1945]
Meeting held in 3-B-24, Sept. 30, 1943. Following persons present:
Walt
Jack Kinney
Bob McCormick
Bill Peet

WALT: *You might want to size up the value of a good screwy chase against this stuff down here . . . second board, bottom row.*

JACK: *That should be feverish as hell. We won't stay on that long. Just a couple of little gags and the gun goes off.*

WALT: Snap it up! *He gets the hot-foot—the tail gag—he runs like hell—the tiger grabs him, and the force pulls them both back. The gun goes off . . . then, the devastated forest. They both go up, but when they hit the ground, they're out . . . right from the explosion. Oh, I see, that's the way you have it here . . . that's your gag.*

This is funny, on your last board. It might be better to take out some of the stuff that might stall.

From the bunny-hug—go right out and into the last board. That second board is the kind of stuff that is liable to stall . . . last row. You have one stop there—the tiger playing with him like a kitten. I was just thinking, what does he do there—tear off the sole of the Goof's shoe? Does he lick his foot? The tiger could just lick his foot, and the Goof is taking it . . . laughing.

JACK: *We could get a close-up of the rough tongue . . . sandpaper effect.*

WALT: *I thought he could just be having fun tickling him. What is he doing there, eating the shoe? [Jack answers, "Yes."] What is the Goof doing where he has him in the pincers hold? I wonder if the Goof could do something to him.*

JACK: *The same idea as the cat and the mouse. We won't have to have much narration. [Walt assents.]*

WALT *[Referring to sketches with camera:] These things are keen. [Referring to map of Africa:] What do you do—just come down on a bunch of eyes? You could come in and come up close on a pair of eyes. Maybe you come to a close-up—here's these eyes, still in the dark—and a match is struck—then reveal the elephant and the Goof. [The Goof is lighting a pipe.] Then, from that, let the lights come on. It's like having them against a dark drop.*

BILL: *There is one technical point—tigers do not inhabit Africa, but it could be India.*

WALT: *Or Indochina . . . or it could just be a screwy jungle map.*

JACK: *We'll get the chatter of the monkeys, etcetera.*

WALT: *Yes, and get birdcalls [demonstrating], caw, caw, caw . . . all kinds of funny sounds. What were you getting on that silent spot? Try twigs breaking now and then, etcetera. Let an echo follow the roar. Then, after that, nothing but silence—a twig could snap here and there. To get silence you need little contrasting things to create suspense, a few little sounds to make it sound silent.*

JACK: *Like a guy listening to his own heartbeat . . . then, when the tiger comes out, you really whip into it.*

WALT: *This is swell stuff—the whole idea. It's swell for the Goof . . . the dope that he is. I like that big fanny on the elephant.*

[Meeting adjourned.]

Later, when I was directing, there was a meeting called for *Ichabod Crane* (1949). As usual, everyone in the unit pitched in and made any last-minute adjustments, such as touching up the story sketches, checking the dialogue, and making sure that each one of the individual sketches was firmly attached to the storyboard with two pushpins, not one, because otherwise they had a tendency to hang every which way, giving the boards an unevenness that looked like a sloppy job. "Not well thought out," as Walt often noted.

These chores accomplished, the chairs were arranged in front of the boards, with enough ashtrays spread around in strategic positions. Then it was time to break for lunch, knowing all was in order.

Of course, some of the guys took off to Alphonse's restaurant for a couple of relaxing drinks and some food, thinking they had time before the two-o'clock meeting. I grabbed a quick bite and beat it outside to play a little volleyball. When I got back, after a shower, I started to rehearse the telling of the boards. It was about one-fifteen, and I was all alone.

Suddenly I heard the unit door bang open, and with a few coughs, Walt made his appearance, quickly sitting in front of the boards and immediately starting to drum his fingers on the chair arm. This was a surefire tip that he was in one of his gorilla moods. Frowning at the empty chairs, he lit a cigarette and said, "Okay, Jack, let's get going. What are you waiting for?"

So I started telling the story, pointing out each sketch with an old pointer. The finger-drumming kept on as, offstage, the unit door opened and the guys, relaxed and laughing, entered the room. By now it was around one-thirty. As each of the various groups gathered, they realized that "man was in the forest" (a line from *Bambi*) as they quietly seated themselves. I bravely continued as if nothing unusual was taking place. There wasn't a sound from the group, other than the occasional cough from Walt and his incessant drumming.

The audience reaction was deadly. Gags that were sure laughs hung there as I tried to carry the losing cause. Finally, toward the end of the sequence, there was a scene where Ichabod was in front of a cracked mirror, primping for the party at the heroine's father's house. After fin-

93

ishing his inspection, he cocks his hat and say, "Ichabod, you handsome devil," then picks up his riding crop and shoves it into his belt.

At this point, I ad-libbed the action, saying, "He sheaths his sword," and acted out the sheathing with the pointer, using my left hand as Ichabod's belt. Well, unfortunately for me, there was a long sliver sticking out of the old pointer, and as I "sheathed" it, the gawddamned thing stuck in my finger. Walt laughed for the first time as I dropped the pointer, cussing like mad, and put my wounded finger in my mouth to stop the blood.

Of course, everybody else laughed too, but not I. The tension was broken, as was the skin on my finger. Walt got to his feet and started out of the room, saying jovially, "Okay, put it into production"—leaving behind a long sigh from the sluggards. As I wrapped my handkerchief over the finger, I thought, "The things you have to do around here to get a laugh."

We dreamed up other, less bloody, schemes to get pictures okayed, too. There was one picture we all believed in and wanted to sell to Walt. It was "All the Short Cats Join In," a sequence in the movie *Make Mine Music* (1946). If Walt saw a situation he liked, you got a quick reaction, such as, "This thing has good possibilities, but it needs tightening, so tighten it up and we'll take another look at it." Then he'd stomp off. So, for this story, we carefully fastened the very rough storyboards with just one pushpin each so that the material looked sloppy. Sure enough, Walt reacted as we'd hoped and we were told to "tighten it up." That we did, with full-color pastels on each drawing and with each drawing precisely hung with four push pins, so that nothing could flutter in the air conditioning. We called Walt, he looked the boards over and okayed the story, saying, "Yeah, yeah, that's it—that's what I meant by tightening up your material." It made a very cute picture.

CHAPTER 5

Sports

The inmates were generally an athletic bunch. Every day at noon we played sports—a lot of times at night as well. We played everything—baseball, football, volleyball, badminton, horseshoes, tennis, golf, boxing, polo, gin rummy, bridge, and poker (with betting, of course). Sometimes we'd go swimming or skin diving.

The guys would get out there and really scream their heads off. We got restless from sitting on our fannies all day long. Sports were a good way to get exercise, and everyone played, including Walt, who had two left feet and was the most uncoordinated SOB you'd ever want to meet. The girls played, too—tennis or golf, mostly.

There were studio teams, and they played other studios. A strong rivalry existed between us and Warner Brothers. Disney's usually beat Warner's. In the early days the intramural teams were the Marrieds and the Singles, but later everybody was married, so we had to mix it up.

Naturally, we were all well versed in the art of gamesmanship.

There were a lot of frustrated ex-jocks among us—guys who played high school football or sandlot baseball and then didn't get to go to college because they had to go to work.

We had our share of college heroes, too: guys like Cotton Warburton, halfback for USC; Laurie Vejar, All-American for Notre Dame; Art Cruickshank from Cal Berkeley; Jack Reeder, who'd played for Dartmouth; and, of course, Dick Kinney, USC Black Fox.

Games were played at noon over at Griffith Park, about a mile from the studio.

C lean Game" Kinney strikes again. Volleyball was another noon pastime.

We played night basketball at the Loyola, Hollywood, and Belmont high school gyms. Not good, but good and dirty . . .

||||||||||||||||||||||||||||||

Then there was polo . . . Disney-style. We could rent horses easily, since California was still cow country in those days. They were mostly just nags.

Walt loved horses. He never had any training, though he had ridden a plow horse on his father's farm. He was always getting bucked off, but that didn't discourage him. He'd dust himself off and try again. Later he finally bought his own string of polo ponies. On weekends he played with guys like Darryl Zanuck from 20th Century-Fox and Will Rogers, who were really quite good.

S ometimes we'd play other kinds of sports on Sundays. Donkey baseball was a fad for a while. You could get donkeys for about fifty cents a day. It was a different game, all right. The object was to swing first, then run over to the donkey, climb up, and try to get to first base. Just staying on was a challenge.

Later, when the studio moved to Burbank, Ping-Pong was played on the cafeteria balcony. We cheated, and that made it more fun.

There was a gym called the Penthouse Club on the roof of one of the Burbank buildings. We went there for wrestling, gymnastics, and weightlifting. There was a restaurant and a sunbathing deck, too.

Carl Johnson, our trainer, was a middleweight wrestling champion, having represented Sweden in the 1912 Olympics. He had a saying, "The outside of a medicine ball is good for the insides of an artist." But that was only one man's opinion.

Once a bunch of the boys from the Cutting Department were tossing film cans around (this was long before Frisbees). One went astray . . .

. . . and interrupted an important putt on the studio putting green.

The ever-stylish guys from the East played, too.

Gull watching" was another popular sport. "Seal rock" (taken from *Seal Island*, the first in the True Life Adventure documentary series), located at the corner of Mickey Mouse Avenue and Dopey Drive, was a gathering place for "barkers." The girls in the Nunnery (the Ink and Paint Department) paraded by on their way to the cafeteria.

Once in a while we'd get together in the sound stage at noon for dancing to our own music. The Fire House Five Plus Two played Dixieland tunes.

Then there were parties at night. Someone would decide to entertain a group of ten or fifteen people at his house. We played charades. Music titles were a favorite.

CHAPTER 6

On to Features

Short subjects were used as sort of a buffer once *Snow White* became such an unqualified success, although they continued to be popular with the public and even garnered several Academy Awards. Animated features were the future, and during the late thirties Walt spent most of his time working on new feature material.

By this time I had been made a Story Director. *The Brave Little Tailor* (1938), my first, won an Academy Award nomination. I was assigned the job of trying to develop Mickey Mouse into more than a supporting character, which wasn't easy, for somehow Mickey had become a straight man to Donald Duck, Goofy, Pluto, and Peg Leg Pete. Walt wanted to give Mick a kick in the ass; he was afraid he was becoming too much of a Boy Scout.

Soon, two more of my stories—*Mickey's Trailer* (1938) and *Society Dog Show* (1939)—were put into production. Then I was assigned to *Pinocchio* (1940)! It was my first feature, although I had contributed a few pieces of business on *Snow White* and had attended several story meetings. I was immensely happy. *Pinocchio* was a challenge. Collodi's book was a bit disjointed as far as animation story content was concerned. I was good at timing chases, so I took the section from where Jiminy Cricket goes underwater in search of Pinocchio to the end of the picture. We had time to develop the story (or so we thought), since *Bambi* was scheduled for production ahead of us.

For lack of space, the *Bambi* unit was moved to Hollywood and into plush quarters, while those of us working on *Pinocchio* were ensconced in those old, beat-up apartment houses—strictly second-team in prestige. Dumb and happy, we went about it as though we knew what we were doing. We were virtually ignored while the push and pressure were being applied to the *Bambi* units. Very little news filtered down to us of the progress being made by the Hollywood-based *Bambi* group.

Then, one day, Walt just kind of walked in on us. A series of story meetings were ordered from Sequence One to the end. And indeed it was the end. *Bambi* was held up, and all hell broke loose. Walt declared us in production. Ben Sharpsteen was assigned as the "whip" or Supervising Producer. Ben was very good at this. He was no prima donna, just a darn good pusher.

I lucked out with my sequences, and as they were being split up between various top-notch direction units—Jaxon, Bill Roberts, Ham Luske, and Fergy—lo and behold, I was kicked up to full-fledged Animation Director.

I was moved, storyboards and all, from our beat-up quarters into Walt's own direction room or "music room"—right next door to his private office. Posh! I was given a large director's desk, my own private moviola, an assistant director (Lou Debney), a secretary, and layout men (Art Heineman, John Hubley, Bruce Bushman, and Dave Rose).

"Crank it out" was the word, so we did. Recording sessions were scheduled for voices, along with live-action staging sessions. By gawd, all I needed to be a bona fide director were puttees, a cap, and a megaphone! I was twenty-six, the youngest director at the studio.

There was only one fly in the ointment. Walt's can and shower had a door leading from his office into mine, and he was wont to drop in unexpectedly and ask, "How's everything going?" A couple times he caught me as I was brown-bagging lunch before going out to play noon baseball. This could be very disconcerting, as I would have to answer his questions with a mouthful of sandwich.

I took to listening to the sound of his toilet flushing and other signs, but sometimes he just burst in without clues. Finally, I solved the problem by pushing the moviola over close to the door so there'd be a loud bump before he could enter the room. After a few of these collisions, Walt started walking around through the proper entrance, the secretary's office. Peace of mind was restored to the unit.

We did a lot of research on *Pinocchio*, and had many meetings to tighten up the story. In an effort to unravel it for animation, the entire story department attended a Saturday matinee of the play at the Wilshire Ebell Club. The good ladies turned out en masse, dressed to the gills, and settled down to enjoy an afternoon of high drama, comedy, pathos, tragedy, and misadventure, starring that unpredictable little wooden puppet whose antics had stirred the imagination of children throughout the world. Unfortunately, however, the players couldn't quite bring it off. By the second act, the audience was failing that dreaded trial known as the "squirm test."

A negative squirm test is one of the most feared audience reactions for all ambitious producers, whether of stage, screen, radio, or TV. Today there are many more sophisticated tests, such as the Nielsen ratings service. But the squirm test is still the most insidious. A failure is easily identified by such clues as seat-squeaking, throat-clearing, foot-shuffling, nervous coughing, rest-room visits, and popcorn-buying. It is also noticeable by the lack of laughter and applause.

In the middle of the act, the tedium was suddenly broken by a surprise attack! An air raid of paper planes was dive-bombing the captive audience! The ladies in picturesque hats were somewhat protected from the descending craft, while those with bared heads were not so fortunate, and were forced to take refuge under their seats or scamper for the lobby. Of course, the play taking place on stage was affected too, and soon the lights went up and the curtain came down. Strangely enough, the bombardment ceased at that juncture.

Having been thus rescued, the guys from the Story Department gathered in the foyer, curious as to the identity of the perpetrator of this audacious attack. The mystery was quickly solved when young Roy Disney, Jr. (now the extremely wealthy head of Walt Disney Productions), sauntered down the stairs from the balcony. Naturally, we knew how to look out for our own and quickly spirited the guilty culprit out of the gracious Ebell Club and into the nearest malt shop, where young Roy admitted that he would have started his attack sooner, except that it had taken the first act and a half to "build" his squadron.

Many new techniques were used on "Pinoke" that hadn't been used on *Snow White*. A model department, created and headed by former story man Joe Grant, turned out three-dimensional scale statuettes of all the characters, and designed mechanical props for things like the stagecoach, and the inside of Monstro the whale, showing his ribs moving as he breathed, which helped the animators.

Gustave Tenggren painted beautiful color illustrations for inspiration, and the incomparable Albert Hurter set the styles and contributed unusual background techniques. Charlie Phillippi acted as color coordinator, and the Ink and Paint Department applied shadows and tints that puffed up the characters' cheeks and gave them a nice feeling of roundness.

Employing this shading technique added to their already painstaking job, and it was never used again. Then all the key sequences were shot, using live-action for rotoscope, a process in which the animators trace over real-life poses for their extremes, loosening them up as they go.

The film was exceptionally well cast, with Dickie Jones as Pinocchio; Walter Catlett and Don Barclay as the Fox and the Cat; and Evelyn Venable and Charley Judels, both well known in motion pictures, as the Blue Fairy and the Evil Coachman. Cliff Edwards, who was a star in his own right as "Ukelele Ike" in the Ziegfeld Follies and who had several records to his credit, did the voice of Jiminy Cricket; and Christian Rub, also a well-known actor, did Geppetto. The song "When You Wish Upon a Star," with music by Leigh Harline, Ned Washington, and Paul Smith, won an Academy Award.

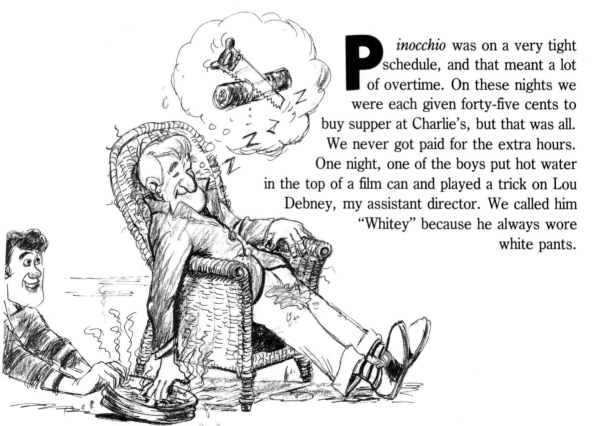

G eppetto was a wonderful character, but Christian Rub was not. He was always cast as a kindly old man because he looked so sweet, but he was really an irascible, nasty old guy. He was always spouting the glories of Hitler . . . until one day we got tired of listening and decided to fix him.

There's a scene in *Pinocchio* where Geppetto is inside the whale's stomach, floating on a raft. When Monstro opens his mouth, a wave of fish floods in and Geppetto runs around like crazy, trying to catch them. Well, during the live-action shooting for that scene, we had Christian up on a makeshift stage and he had to pretend he was catching fish while the raft was being jostled. There were five or six grips in place, big strong guys, ready to "rock the boat" and create the desired effect. They gave Christian a ride he'd never forget.

P *inocchio* was on a very tight schedule, and that meant a lot of overtime. On these nights we were each given forty-five cents to buy supper at Charlie's, but that was all. We never got paid for the extra hours. One night, one of the boys put hot water in the top of a film can and played a trick on Lou Debney, my assistant director. We called him "Whitey" because he always wore white pants.

When *Pinocchio* was in the can and ready for distribution, there was a gala premiere at the Hollywood Pantages Theater, with searchlights, stars, press, red carpets, the whole shebang. Everyone who worked on the picture was given free ducats to the command performance, so we all rushed out to rent tuxedos.

Of course, none of them really fit, and you've never seen a more uncomfortable-looking group of slobs, except for Bruce Bushman (son of Francis X. Bushman, hearthrob of silent movies and a star of the original *Ben Hur*). *He* made a grand entrance in his very own tails. He was "to the manor born" and looked it, while the rest of us tried to keep our stiff shirts and collars in place, sweating out the whole ordeal.

With *Pinocchio* finished, I was reassigned as a Director of Shorts. So it was back to the apartment houses and the Story Department.

The first short subject I made as a Director was *Bone Trouble* (1940), starring Pluto and Butch, the bulldog. We got ourselves a good story. John Hubley and Don Griffith were assigned as layout men, Lou Debney as assistant director, and Frank Churchill did the music.

In those days, when the rough pencil tests were completed, we always had a showing for the entire studio personnel in the sound stage. This usually took place at noon, and not on "company time."

These "sneak previews" were real sweating-it-out ordeals and often determined the fate of the particular shorts unit involved. Besides cutting an acetate record of the audible audience reaction, Walt asked each viewer to fill out a form. On *Bone Trouble* we had a particularly fine reaction. Our spirits soared. We were up and our budget was under! This was unusual, so everybody was happy, including Walt and Roy.

During this time, several abortive attempts were made to unionize the studio. The motive was there. Salaries, for the most part, were on the low side for the assistants and junior animators. Screen credits on shorts were not allowed except for Walt Disney's name, whereas all the other studios had been giving credits for years. The studio was adamant on this subject, feeling that all the credit should belong to Walt. This rankled the workers, especially when the general public believed that Walt did everything—animation, ink and paint, backgrounds, layout, voices, and music. Trouble in paradise.

Then we were told that it was now time to move to the new studio in Burbank, way out in the San Fernando Valley. From our previous ten or twelve acres we went to a whopping fifty-three, around half of the Black Fox Military Academy's polo field, right smack in the middle of nowhere. The move was completed with minimal fuss. About the only personal treasures we were able to salvage for our new quarters were our coffeepots! Thus began a new era. But not without typical fireworks.

To show goodwill, the studio arranged a weekend celebration party at the Lake Naraconian Club. Of course, we had to pay for our own room and board. The event was very well organized by Hal Adelquist and his helpers, who arranged many activities for all to enjoy—swimming, horseshoes, baseball, volleyball, touch football, aquaplaning, Ping-Pong, and, of course, boozin'!

Handsome cups, inscribed "Walt's Field Day," were awarded to the winners of these various events except for boozin', and there were just too many competitors in that last event to declare a winner. However, if one had been awarded, Fred Moore would have won hands down. He performed a very classical high dive off a second-story balcony and wasn't hurt a bit.

It was a bash to end all bashes, needless to say.

Soon, everything was coming up roses. The product was well received all around the world. *Pinocchio* was released, *Fantasia* was in the mill, and *Bambi* was getting ready for production, in addition to all the shorts being turned out to fill the program.

The new studio was like a college campus with a country-club atmosphere. Traffic boys were at our beck and call.

After finishing *Bone Trouble,* I was assigned to story and direction on *Bambi.* There was now a big push to get the picture out. I was briefed by Perce Pearce, the producer, who was often referred to by unbelievers as the biggest flimflammer to rise from the ranks. Perce had started as a lowly inbetweener, but by dint of research (stealing gags), a jolly ho-ho laugh, twinkling blue eyes, an inflappable ego, a manner of speaking up in open story meetings, and other ploys, he had managed to get himself transferred to the Story Department.

His bag chance came when Merrill De Maris, a very competent writer, was faced with an impossible situation. He had been told he would have a special story meeting with Walt on his *Snow White* sequence. Merrill was prepared. His story and boards were in fine, showable shape, but Merrill was a very tense guy, with a terrible inferiority complex. He stewed for three days about having to present his boards to Walt for approval. All the guys in the Story Department assured Merrill that he would have no problems whatsoever, since his material was excellent, but the assurances helped Merrill not one whit. Time was running out. Then came a last-minute reprieve. Perce Pearce unselfishly offered to tell the story for Merrill. Merrill's relief knew no bounds.

All the directors, Dave Hand, the story guys, and Walt assembled in the big sweatbox for the evening meeting. (Most story meetings were scheduled for seven o'clock to save production time.) Merrill sat in the back row. Perce stepped forward with a jolly ho-ho and a twinkle in his eye and gave a performance such as had never before been seen in a Disney story meeting. Every stop was pulled, every dramatic gesture used, each line of dialogue delivered with the proper reading and subtle nuances—a tremendous act! Naturally the sequence was accepted. Walt was enthralled and Perce was installed.

Now I was once again in the presence of this phenom. We were alone. The curtains were drawn so the room was in semidarkness. Perce told me the story of *Bambi* as it had never been told before. I was as amazed by this beautiful ham as Walt had been when Perce gave his *Snow White* performance.

I started the following day in the hallowed precincts of the *Bambi* unit, ensconced in a large room on the third floor. Our assignment was to do the opening sequences. We started as we usually did, by throwing rough sketches up on the storyboards as we felt our way into the continuity, acting out each piece of business for the animators.

After a couple of weeks, during which we were visited several times by other members of the unit, Dave Hand dropped in and said what we were doing was fine for some things, but in the *Bambi* unit each story sketch had to be done as a finished piece of art. "But," he told us, "don't let that stop you, just keep on going as you are, and we'll have some of our story sketch guys follow you up. I gotta get this picture moving into production. Walt wants it ready by Christmas."

Soon after, guys like Marc Davis, Clair Weeks, and Tom Codrick began coming in and snatching our rough sketches off the wall. They returned beautifully rendered sketches to replace the roughs. These finished drawings were each matted in black, with the number pasted on the lower right-hand corner; the scene description and/or dialogue was typewritten and fastened to the matte just below the drawing; and not only that, but each drawing was firmly fastened to the storyboard by *four* pushpins, one in each corner. This was all right with us, as it made our efforts look good, real good. But the expense! I was told not to worry about that, because *Bambi* was strictly first-cabin.

Several weeks went by, and the story and storyboards were taking shape—and what a shape! Every drawing was worthy of framing and hanging in your home, or in an art gallery for that matter.

I informed Dave's production office that we were ready for a meeting with Walt, but was told that first we had to have a review with Dave Hand and Perce Pearce. "Okay, how about sometime next week?" I said. The secretary said, "I'll see what I can do. They have a very tight schedule."

We waited and waited. Eventually, an evening meeting was arranged. Starting at seven o'clock, I got to tell the story. There were six boards filled with drawings for the opening sequence of the picture. I had gotten past the opening pan and as far as drawing No. 8 on the first board when I was interrupted by a jolly ho-ho from Perce Pearce.

Perce stood up, a commanding figure, very carefully buttoned his double-breasted coat, puffed on his pipe, and started toward the storyboard, then retreated toward a box of matches. He again strolled toward the storyboard, pointing toward drawing No. 1 with the stem of his pipe. Inserting the stem of his pipe into his mouth, he scratched the lucifer on the side of the box, started the match toward his pipe, then raised the burning match in the direction of the storyboard and drawing No. 1.

My God, I thought, he's going to set fire to it! Luckily the match burned out before it reached the board. Naturally, Perce had to return the burnt match to an inconvenient ashtray. He again approached the storyboard, but as he arrived his double-breasted coat was again unbuttoned! Slowly and methodically, Perce rebuttoned the garment.

Now, with a jolly ho-ho and a few *ahems,* he was ready. "I've been thinking . . ." Pause. He pointed to drawing No. 1, then carefully walked from drawing No. 1 to drawing No. 8 . . . stopped in front of drawing No. 8, gave it extremely close scrutiny, then retraced his steps to drawing No. 1. A long pause, then, "I've been thinking . . . "Pause . . . "Whether . . ." Now he turned to his audience and paused (dramatic) . . . "I've been thinking . . ." And then, with a rush, comparatively speaking, "whether drawing number one would be better in drawing number four's spot and then drawing number three in place of number two, thus moving number seven into the number-one spot, followed by number seven here . . . number eight there, and number six . . . no, that won't work."

At this point, several other persons spoke up, each with a different combination of positions for drawings No. 1 through No. 8. You'd be surprised how many combinations can be made from only eight drawings. The argument continued until 10:00 P.M. At that point the Unit Manager, who had not entered into the discussion (neither had I), announced, "Hey, fellas, it's ten o'clock." Suddenly the discussion stopped. "Why, so it is," said an astonished Perce. "Let's leave it this way and have a further discussion." Then, with a jolly ho-ho and a twinkle in his eye, he announced, "Tomorrow's a working day!" A few more jolly ho-hos, and the meeting dispersed. It was just about the most frustrating day of my life.

119

Two weeks later there was a second story meeting. This time I hoped to tell the entire sequence, past drawing No. 8.

The sequence began by introducing all of nature's cute creatures—most of them recently born to proud parents—and of course ending with the newborn Bambi and his mother. The dialogue was "Bambi . . . Bambi . . . my little Bambi." That's all. There were many storyboards, with hundreds of story sketches, following this introduction of our hero, but we never got to them to find out if the continuity was working. The meeting stopped for a profound discussion of how the immortal line should be delivered. Perce advocated that it should be delivered this way: "Bam . . . beeee . . . (long pause) . . . Bammmm . . . beee . . . my . . . litt . . . tullll . . . . Baammm . . . beeeeeeeeee . . ." He held center stage in front of drawing No. 16, which depicted the "mother and child" cushioned on a soft bower of leaves and branches, with the gentle sunlight filtering through the boughs of the trees, spotlighting the scene—somewhat like a depiction of the Nativity. On finishing his emotional rendition, Perce blew his nose and gently dabbed at his eyes. Not a sound was made by the group until Perce was comfortably seated. Then Larry Morey (a fine lyricist) spoke: "Percie . . . I would like to make a suggestion . . ." Perce graciously nodded his agreement while lighting his pipe with an ordinary kitchen match (which always burned out before it made contact with the pipe bowl). Larry's rendition went something like this: "Bam-bi . . . Bambi . . . my . . . lit-tle . . . Bam-beeeee . . . " After Larry's reading, Perce again presented his dramatic reading. But Larry was not about to give up. "Yes, Percie, I see your point, but a most important overall fact must be faced: one, this is the first line spoken in the picture; two, this line of dialogue establishes the fact that animals *will* talk in the picture, and, three, thematically I want to sneak in an oboe obbligato with a flute overtone to augment the dialogue and mood." The polite argument continued until 10:00 P.M. when the participants agreed that they would sleep on it.

The next working day, I called Ben Sharpsteen and asked to see him. Walking into his office, I burst out, "Ben, for chrissake get me off that goddam *Bambi*, onto shorts, anything." And that's how I got back to normal again, and back to shorts and Goofy.

CHAPTER 7

Back to Shorts

My decision to bail out of the *Bambi* fiasco came at a very good time. Management had just made a big decision to set up individual production units for each character in the Disney menagerie. Using a number of the characters in one film tied up a lot of valuable talent, and only one film resulted. But if each group of creative people developed expertise in handling one character and worked on films starring just that one character, better productions would result, at less cost.

The new units were set up—Jack King handled the Ducks, Norm Ferguson and Nick Nichols the Plutos, and Bill Roberts and Riley Thomson the Mickeys. The Goofy series, luckily, came to me. I was happy to work with Goofy. He was tall, lean, and gangly, and you could get a lot of good poses out of him. You could even tie him up in knots. That wasn't true of Mickey or the Ducks, who couldn't be distorted. I liked Goofy's character, too. He didn't have a worry in the world, just took things as they were. He was very philosophical.

For my unit, I drew a Class A team from the studio talent pool: Ralph Wright, a keen story and gag man with a peculiar sense of humor that fit right in with the Goof's oddball antics; Lou Debney as my assistant director; and Woolie Reitherman and John Sibley as my lead animators. All told, we made up a competitive, on-the-ball team that was perfect for turning out shorts of the kind I had planned for Goofy.

Every Friday, all directors were required to give Walt an interoffice communication report for him to read over the weekend. I submitted my ideas for this new Goofy series. The "how-to" format opened up a vast area. The subject matter could be anything; do-it-yourself repairs, or even the wide world of sports, all open to Goofy's dum-dum exploration. What he would do in any given story would be the hook we'd hang it on.

The following Monday, I got a call from Walt, who said, "Jack, this is one hell of an idea! Go ahead on it!"

Encouraged by Walt's favorable reaction (this didn't happen every time), I asked, "Which one first?"

"Any one of 'em," he said. "Which do you like?"

Knowing of Walt's keen interest in polo, I said, "How about *How to Ride a Horse?*"

"Great! Go on that one!"

And that's how the Goof's "how-to" series got started—a series that ran for about two dozen episodes before Goofy went into his last caroming, crashing pratfall.

‖‖‖‖‖‖‖‖‖‖‖‖‖‖‖‖‖‖‖‖‖‖‖‖

Another member of our group who contributed an invaluable bit to the development of the series was John McLeish. And believe me, no one else could have been substituted.

As production took its natural course, I did voice casting for a narrator to do the voice-over dialogue. I was looking for something different. Voice-over was the only choice, because, as we saw it, the Goof couldn't talk much, if at all. The reason for this was that Pinto Colvig, the old circus hand who had done Goofy's patter for years, had left the studio. Consequently, all the Goof's manic mutterings had to be lifted from the studio library of sound tracks. Voice-over was our crutch—but a special kind of crutch! We needed a voice that would be completely at variance with what was happening on the screen, the screwy situations that only Goofy could get into. We wanted someone who could project a heavy, omniscient quality, straight and pontifical, no matter what our gonged-out hero was doing. I put a lot of Hollywood voice boxes over the jumps—radio, stage, and film speechifiers by the dozen—but none of them came over with exactly what I was looking for. It was then that I discovered John McLeish.

McLeish had been scooped up in Disney's worldwide talent search, and John had plenty of that. He was a top-flight artist, an excellent draftsman with a highly developed sense of color. Like everyone else, he was put through the studio production grinder, ending up as a story sketch man on feature films. One of John's outstanding attributes was his devotion to the legitimate theater in all its forms, and he had a special fixation on John Barrymore, to whom he bore a certain resemblance. He added to that resemblance by wearing longish hair in the Barrymore pompadour, a romantic mustache, and shirts with long collar points, the kind known as "Barrymore." His face was long, with a finely chiseled nose, which added to the resemblance, too. John generally conducted himself as his own inimitable version of the Great Profile, even while he was doing everyday, ordinary things. Most acquaintances claimed he was even better than the original.

But McLeish's truly outstanding characteristic was his voice, to which he gave full play at the drop of a buskin. Cultivated, deep, and resonant, John's dextrous set of pipes was often displayed for the benefit and awe of fellow workers. During long sessions at the drawing boards, when he would utter imposing passages from the Immortal Bard, all was delivered in the most fulsome Barrymore fashion, every syllable, word, and phrase rolling forth in sonorous or thunderous tones that shook his listeners, and the windows. Such dramatic vocal ability did not long go hidden under a bushel in the Disney Studio of that period. The trolls, elves, and pixies were always encouraged to don different bonnets; interchangeability kept production costs down.

Somehow, through a leaky spout in the studio pipeline, word trickled down to me of this fantastic pencil pusher who could do Barrymore better than Barrymore himself. Maybe this bird was the very one I'd had my net out for. So I had John over to the sound stage for a session. History was made that day.

What I didn't tell John before the recording began was our idea of doing a straight voice to contrast with the wacky visuals. Knowing of John's tendency to ham it up on occasion, I was afraid he'd overdo it and lose the cutting edge of our idea. Instead, I told him to give it a straight reading, all seriousness, just as though he were narrating an educational or documentary film.

John nodded in agreement. Serious, man!

He frowned deeply, adjusted the Windsor knot in his tie, checked his script, inhaled deeply, and took off right on cue. Ah, there was a performance that even the Great Profile would have been proud of. There wasn't a dry eye on that sound stage when John rumbled into his finale.

We had our voice, indeed! John bowed to our plaudits with becoming modesty. He thought of his narration as pure drama, and I didn't tell him different. To do so would have crushed him. But after a few pictures had been made in this style, John found out and felt that he had been duped. He felt that he'd wasted his talents on what he referred to as "that anthropomorphic nonentity," Goofy. In later sessions, John tried to be funny, which would have killed the basic premise of contrast, and we had to work hard to keep his delivery straight and pompous.

T he formula we'd developed, the contrast of voice and action, was a good one, and in *How to Ride a Horse* we played it full out. Goofy, dressed in typically ill-fitting English riding clothes, rides to the hounds as McLeish's supercilious voice gives instructions. With John's rotund descriptions rolling over him, Goofy blissfully demonstrates some of the most ridiculous horsemanship seen since man first bestrode a shaggy prehistoric nag. And, for the first time in a cartoon, we used a device that worked wonders in later pictures: a slow-motion demonstration of how to do whatever the Goof was maddeningly lousing up.

The basic idea and its masterful execution by the animators made this series a winner right from the start. *How to Ride a Horse* was so well received by the distributor, RKO, that it was included in the feature film *The Reluctant Dragon* (1941), instead of being released as a short subject.

That "horse opera" having done so well, we continued with *The Art of Self-Defense* (1941), *The Olympic Champ* (1942), and *How to Play Football* (1944). The interplay between John McLeish's narration and Goofy's antics was a delight to audiences for the run of the series, and we were just as delighted in making them.

Earlier in the book, a transcript of a story meeting from *Tiger Trouble* (1945), one of my all-time favorite Goofy shorts, shows what it was like in story meetings with Walt. Well, Walt okayed that picture pretty much as it was. "But," he said, "try to get rid of those stripes, they're too costly." (Stripes are very meticulous work for the Ink and Paint Department, because if they aren't exact they waver and attract your eye from the action.) Eliminating stripes isn't easy when your picture's about a tiger. But it gave me an idea.

In the last scene, the tiger is chasing the Goof, who's riding in a howdah on the back of the elephant—and the elephant falls on the tiger, smashing him flat. When the elephant gets up and disappears into the jungle, the tiger's stripes are stuck on his fanny. Then the poor tiger gets up, looks down, and covers his stripeless body as though he were suddenly nude. When Walt saw the picture, he said, "Well, you got rid of the stripes . . . in the last scene." It made such a cute ending, he was happy anyway.

〰〰〰〰〰〰〰〰〰〰

We had a certain amount of freedom in the Shorts units. Of course, Walt had to okay every picture, but it was possible to trick him now and then, as I mentioned earlier.

During the early forties, Walt went to South America, and when he got back he told reporters that he had flown over "a jungle so thick, the hand of man had never set foot in it." I used that line in *Tiger Trouble,* and as far as I know, Walt never caught on.

We fought back in other ways, too. The lack of screen credits at Disney's was a continual sore point, but I got us into three of my pictures: *How to Play Baseball* (1942), *How to Play Football* (1944), and *Hockey Homicide* (1945). Look for "Clean Game" Kinney, Fearless Ferguson, Swivelhips Smith, Moose Williams, and Chief Geronimi among the players.

These shorts were just the way I liked 'em—loud and fast, with continuous dialogue. I threw everything in but the kitchen sink.

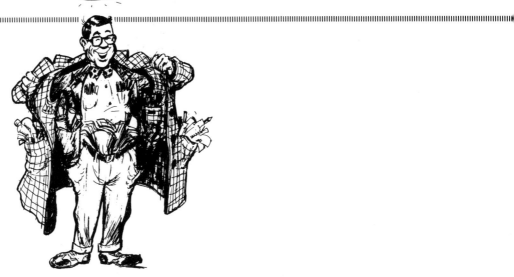

John Sibley was the best "Goof" man in the business—a damn funny guy and a good animator. He was a pleasure to know and a joy to work with, and I believe he enjoyed every frame of every Goof picture from *How to Ride a Horse* to *Motormania*.

John was about as uninhibited as any of us, and he had a very broad sense of humor. The only thing he took seriously was the Notre Dame football team, because he was from South Bend, Indiana. But even John could be surprised.

Late one afternoon, during the rainy season, John and I walked into our cohort Bob Beemiller's room to check with him on a scene. It was close to five and Bob was getting his rain gear on, ready to brave the elements. Among other preparations we inadvertently observed, Bob was filling his pockets with pushpins, erasers, pencils, and animation paper, and he was wrapping background paper around his midsection, before putting on his overcoat.

He didn't mind us.

"My God," Sibley exclaimed, "what in hell are you doing, Bob?"

"Well," said Bob, "I've got a little outside job to do for a friend of mine."

"Oh" we said, "what kind of a picture are you working on?"

"Religious film," said Bob,

John and I thought that was about the funniest thing we'd ever heard. **127**

About this time, Dick Kinney, Milt Schaffer, and I were putting together a short called *Motormania*, based on a traffic-safety theme, with Goofy playing a Jekyll-and-Hyde role as Mr. Walker and Mr. Wheeler. We consulted the National Safety Council and the Los Angeles Police Traffic Department for expert advice.

Mr. Walker was a nice average man until he got behind the wheel. Then he became Mr. Wheeler, a maniac driver and public menace. We had just had a meeting with Walt, and he'd okayed the picture for production. We were sitting around, chewing it over, trying to think of someone to do the narration, and I had just said, "Gawd! I wish John McLeish was in town. He'd be perfect," when, as if on cue, the phone rang. It was John, calling from New York.

"McLeish!" I shouted into the phone. "I wish you were here!"

"I shall be," he intoned, "if you've got a job for me."

"You got it."

"I'll be there Monday."

So we set up a recording date. John did a masterful job and was assigned the narration. Also at that time, the studio began hiring story sketch guys for the television commercial unit—and John had his job.

All went well for a spell until John moved in and set up housekeeping in his office. One day the commercial clients dropped in to check the various storyboards, and John was literally caught with his pants down. He was changing into clean shorts and a shirt, off the wash line that he'd strung up across the room, festooned with socks, shirts, and shorts, some of which were still dripping.

"Come in, come in," said John in his grand manner, as he parted the clothes to allow them to enter.

John showed the clients his storyboards. They were satisfied with his presentation, but the woman in charge of the Commercials Department was incensed, irate, and beside herself. She demanded that John be fired at once. John had been fired before, so he knew what to do. He packed his personal belongings into cartons and paper bags.

Before leaving the premises, he stopped outside Walt's office and sang his swan song in his inimitable voice—a classic from *Snow White,* "Some Day My Prince Will Come." It was a lovely, resonant rendition that elicited appreciative applause from all the inmates, but no acknowledgment from Walt's office except the appearance of the studio guards to escort John out the gates.

Our Goof unit kept cranking out pictures—all under budget and ahead of schedule. We were rewarded for our efforts with bonuses based on a rating system of A, B, and C for excellence, depending on audience reaction. Our crew collected bonus checks on every picture. We were a happy group, having fun and picking up some welcome bucks besides!

Soon everyone got into the act. Competition got fiercer and fiercer. Some of the shorts animators were cleaning up—Fred Spencer, Ed Love, and John Sibley, to name a few. Quality was the key, and Walt rated every picture personally.

Then came the rumbles and grumbles from those poor souls not included in this bonus windfall, namely the people assigned to features. They were jealous. Finally they broke through. The bonus system was scratched and nobody won, especially the studio. From $35,000 per picture, including the bonus payoffs, the budgets grew and grew—$45,000, $60,000, $70,000. There must be a moral to this. I guess you could call it incentive. (Later the cost rose so high that shorts were priced right out of existence.)

<hr>

The studio continued to concentrate on features, with *Dumbo* (1941), *Bambi* (1942), and *Peter Pan* (1953) in story and *The Mickey Feature* in production (later made part of *Fun and Fancy Free* and released in 1947).

There was an intense rivalry going on among studios. Warner Brothers, Screen Gems, MGM, Harman-Ising, Walter Lantz, UPA, and Disney's were tops at the time, so they were the ones to beat, despite disparities in budget and staff.

A lot of the guys at the other studios would say, "We wish (*sob*) we had the chance to do good things like they do with big budgets. . . ." But many of us wished we had the freedom they had. Also, some of the smaller studios had people working for them who could compete with anyone, and they made some damn funny pictures—uninhibited, fresh, not worked over too much, as happened sometimes at Disney's at that time.

CHAPTER 8

The Frenetic Forties

Sixteen frames to the foot, twenty-four frames per second—those measurements are the animator's rule for timing action and tempo. After nearly ten years working with exposure sheets, it became second nature to think in those terms.

In 1940 I built a house in the hills above Burbank, just three miles from the studio. In fact, I could look down and see the studio from my backyard.

I had planned for some time to build a sun shelter out back by my swimming pool. I had the uncut lumber ready, and early one Saturday morning I emerged with my pencil and power saw, and set about carefully measuring the cross-pieces in two-foot segments, following my hand-drawn design. I knew exactly how many pieces I needed to cut, and soon it was finished. But, lo! I was short. I checked my figures—sixteen to the foot, thirty-two for two feet, right? Wrong! I had inadvertently used film footage inches. I tried to recall my early school days, when twelve inches equaled a foot and not sixteen frames, but after recutting the wood, I was left with a pile of short ends suitable only for firewood. For better or for worse, the cartoon business was in my blood.

|||||||||||||||||||||||||||||

Others decided to leave the business behind and go on to other things. Ray Kelly was one.

Ray came from New York and started at Disney's as a story man. One day he decided to become a priest. He went to Santa Clara and was ordained as a Jesuit. He'd come back now and then to say hello, and one time "The Irish contingent"—Ted Sears, Harry Reeves, Fergy, and me—took him to lunch.

Ted told him the story of the Pope and the traveling salesman. As I remember it, the traveling salesman wants to make a deal with the Pope. He offers him 10,000 pazoozas, but the Pope says no. He goes to 15,000, 20,000, and finally 25,000 pazoozas. The Pope is really sweating it out. He realizes that the money could help fix cracks in the Sistine Chapel, steam-clean St. Peter's façade, and plant more shrubbery, but finally he turns down the generous offer.

Well, the bishops see all this, and want to know what's going on. Finally the Pope tells them: the traveling salesman had wanted him to insert the word "Coca-Cola" into the mass in place of *Dominus vobiscum.*

About a year later, Father Kelly said his first mass at the Blessed Sacrament Church which we all attended. After mass we went over to congratulate him, and he confessed that every time he came to say *Dominus vobiscum* he thought of Coca-Cola. We all agreed that once a gag man, always a gag man.

ıııııııııııııııııııııııı

Speaking of humor, just what is it? It's an intangible thing—hard to capture, hard to create—yet it's all around us. We all know the difference between subtle humor and slapstick. Well, cartoon humor combines all of it, from titters to belly laughs. All in all, humor is a fine gem to be cherished and shared, never forced or faked, like laugh tracks in so many TV programs, which I resent like a poke in the ribs. I believe that laughter is strictly up to each individual, like religion. It can't be analyzed, just enjoyed.

This true story is better than many gags:

"You're paying two bucks a bag for manure? Come on over to my place after work and I'll give you all the manure you want for nothin'." It was animator Riley Thomson talking to my buddy Roy Williams. Riley raised horses, and Roy was putting in a new lawn.

"Swell," says Roy. "I'll follow you home with my truck." It's summertime in Burbank, and that means hot. So naturally Roy and Riley have to have a few cool drinks to prepare themselves for pitching horse manure. Then, after a few more drinks, the sun goes down and the boys get themselves to the corral. By nine o'clock Roy's pickup truck is loaded to overflowing.

"Thanks, Rile," says Roy as he drives off with the finest grade-A horseshit available.

Now Roy's in a bit of a hurry to get home and spread the manure on the new lawn, so naturally he speeds up his machine and naturally one of Burbank's finest pulls him over to the curb and presents him with a ticket, after which Roy is not only in a hurry but kind of mad too as he turns into his street. He careens the car just a mite too much . . . C-R-R-ACK! He breaks an axle and has to find a tow truck to pull his disabled automobile the rest of the way home.

Arriving finally around midnight, he spreads his free manure all over his nice new fresh lawn. A job well done!

Roy gets to bed around 1:30 A.M. and sleeps like a log. In fact, he oversleeps like a log. Around 10:30 A.M., he is awakened by loud knocking and yelling. His neighbors have come to call upon him, vociferously demanding he get off his fat ass and remove the manure from the neighborhood. Roy agrees, inasmuch as the friendly natives threaten to call the law unless he complies.

By noon he is able to pick up his repaired truck. And by two o'clock in the afternoon he has scraped all of the offending stench from his lawn. But where has his lawn disappeared to? It's burnt out. The strength of the thoroughbred manure has proved too much for the tender young shoots.

Driving to the local dump, Roy counts his blessings. Total savings on packaged manure, twelve dollars. Cost of traffic ticket, fifteen dollars. Tow charge, $7.50. New axle, $32.50, and labor $22.50 additional. A one-dollar charge at the dump plus the cost of reseeding and pampering his lawn, another $7.50 or eight dollars. All told, it amounts to roughly $86.13, less the twelve-dollar savings on the original store-bought manure, which brings it down to only $74.13 plus tax; not bad for a summer evening's work. However, Roy learned a truth that remained in his mind for years to come: "Never look a gift horse in the rear end!"

One day after a game of softball and a shower in the Penthouse
Club, Roy got on the scales. John Sibley couldn't get over the
result.

Walt's brother Ray was a familiar sight in the 1940s. He lived a few blocks from the studio in Burbank and often came around to sell insurance. The kickstand on his bike was loose and it made a helluva racket, but he didn't care as long as he saved gas. You could hear him coming for miles.

Ray had a lot of customers at the studio. They bought from him because they thought it would get them in good with Walt. Ray's prices were none too cheap, though, and when people saw that Walt couldn't care less, many canceled their policies.

General unrest at the studio—owing to low wages for assistants and no screen credits, among other poor conditions—led to a lot of talk about unionizing. Several cartoon studios had already joined and were reaping the benefits. It was spring of 1941, and the Depression seemed to be over. Prosperity was just around the corner, and a lot of the people at Disney's wanted to turn that corner. Arguments for and against the union echoed through the halls. Sides were drawn up, meetings were held, and then, along about May, the studio went on strike.

A picket line went up at the studio gates. Picket signs saying things like DISNEY UNFAIR were artistically composed. Gunther Lessing, the company attorney, was hung in effigy. Cries of "fink," "scab," and other epithets were hurled against the nonstrikers, who retaliated by calling strikers "commies." It was a mess.

Those of us who crossed the picket line were in shock. We were naive, having never been exposed to the workings of capital and labor. That first day was a long one. It was hot out, damned hot. The pickets sweltered, and the people on the inside sweltered, too. Along about four o'clock a few of us were told to come up to Walt's office. At last, word from higher up.

||||||||||||||||||||||||||

Walt had hired a photographer to take pictures of the people on the picket line, and now these photos—blown up to poster size—lined the walls of his office. They were huge things that made each person exceptionally identifiable.

Walt walked around the room, peering intently at each picture. Pointing his finger, he said things like "Damn, I didn't think *he'd* go against me"; "That sonofabitch, I trusted him and he went out on me"; "It figures"; "What's his gripe?"; or "We can get along without him." We got the uneasy feeling that he was filing his feelings away in his prodigious memory for some future revenge.

When Lessing arrived with Roy Disney, Walt said, "Well, how long do you think it will last, Gunny?"

Gunther answered cockily, "It'll be over in twenty-four hours." This news was acclaimed by all present and served as a wonderful lift to our spirits. Walt broke out a few bottles of Harvey's Bristol Cream and we all sat down to celebrate.

The next day we returned to work, thinking that the strike would blow over in a short time. Production went on—and so did the picket line.

Lessing was wrong, but that was no surprise. He was a terribly egotistical guy and a very poor attorney. He only got the job in the first place because he loaned Walt money when he was starting out. Lessing represented the company through the long weeks of the strike, and as usual he managed beautifully to louse everything up. When it was clear that his prediction was way off, he tried to form a *company* union—which soon turned the air blue with maledictions.

The strike became very bitter. Long friendships between "ins" and "outs" were destroyed. The hostility was brutal. Strikers let air out of tires or took screwdrivers and scratched the cars as they drove through the gate. There were fights, even some shots were fired. I was exempt from this treatment because, as a director, I wasn't eligible to join anyway. I had friends on the outside and on the inside.

Mostly it was the inbetweeners, assistants, inkers, and painters who went out, though there were exceptions. Art Babbitt was a top animator, and he became the union leader. He and Bill Tytla were friends, and Bill went out, too. Bill was a big, burly guy, bowlegged, a Russian Cossack who loved horses. He was one of the best animators the studio had. He did the "Night on Bald Mountain" segment of *Fantasia*, with the devil in it. After the strike he went back to New York and never returned.

The union situation was very complicated. There were a couple of gangsters out of Chicago running a lot of the unions in those days—Willie Bioff and George Browne—and of course they didn't like upstarts such as the Screen Cartoonists Guild operating outside their control. Then Warner's went out at the same time. Later some of those guys were blacklisted and never worked in the industry again. In the end, the federal government got involved and the union was installed.

Disney's was required to bring a certain number of people back, but Walt never forgave them. He eventually fired every single one.

Art Babbitt came back, but he and Walt hated each other's guts. Babbitt was a Goofy man, so he ended up with me. I'd run into Walt in the hall and he'd say, "How's Babbitt making out?" "Oh, fine," I'd tell him. "Well, if he gets in your way, let me know!"

They fired Art more than once, but he always got back in. He took his case all the way to the Supreme Court—and won a huge settlement—but then he decided not to stay on after all. He eventually started his own studio and won more than eighty awards for commercials he produced and animated.

The studio was never the same when it was over. Walt cut off all privileges, and Disney's became a very hard-nosed place.

||||||||||||||||||||||||||

During the strike negotiations, the studio decided that it would be best to get Walt out of town. About this time, the State Department had instituted a "Good Neighbor Policy" to create a good relationship between the United States and our friends to the south. They encouraged Walt to go to South America, which he did, along with a handful of studio people. Going back and forth several times, they studied the culture and drew sketches of the people, clothes, and so on that were used for *Saludo Amigos* (1943) and *The Three Caballeros* (1945).

While Walt was away on these trips, we were hard at work on *Dumbo*, which turned out to be one of the cutest, most entertaining pictures Disney's ever made. I directed the pink elephant scene, which was wonderfully animated by Howard Swift, and the black crow sequence.

In this sequence, Dumbo gets smashed on champagne, and wakes up in a tree with a hangover. He doesn't know how he got there, or how to get down. His little friend Timothy the mouse convinces him that he can fly, and he does, but he lands with a big thump. This makes the crows laugh and they do a delightful song called "When I See an Elephant Fly," sung by Cliff Edwards, who also did the voice of Jiminy Cricket.

For some reason, Walt never liked *Dumbo*. I think it was because he wasn't around when we were making it, and of course we ended up with a great picture that came in way under budget.

The next thing we knew, the war was a lot closer than we'd thought. Many of the men and women at the studio enlisted. Others were drafted, and still others were exempt because of age or dependents. The cartoon industry swung quickly into producing training films, and soon the studio was dotted with uniforms of all kinds.

The marines landed (one squadron was stationed right on the premises), along with the air force, coast guard, and navy (sailors *and* fliers). And they all had their advisers, propagandists, writers, editors, etc. Even the British sent over several advisers. Ex–motion picture people, including Frank Capra, were attached to these units, too, working side by side with the more seasoned combat veterans.

The training films being produced starred Disney characters—Mickey, Donald, Goofy—and covered every possible subject. There was a whole series on the "Rules of the Nautical Road," for instance,—how one ship should pass another. One of the military training experts told me that they experimented with two groups of soldiers—one group who read the usual written material for several weeks, and one group who viewed a training film just once. Those watching the pictures passed with a rating 20 percent higher than the readers.

The joint was really jumping. All the rooms were filled. Rationing was in effect—for gas, meat, cigarettes, clothes, tires, butter, and booze. We all had ID cards that had to be carried at all times.

Then there were air-raid drills. Wardens were assigned to go around and make sure we all pulled our blinds down tight so no light could come in while we waited for the "all clear." People didn't know what to think. We'd never been through anything like it. It was a jittery time—a scary time, really—especially for everyone along the coast.

I was assigned to the camouflage unit. My first job was to come up with a clever idea for how to camouflage Boulder Dam and hide Lake Mead from prying enemy eyes. This was easier said than done. I pondered the problem, got out the plaster of Paris, and made a scale model. Nothing doing. There were many ideas considered. Luckily, Boulder Dam is still standing.

My next assignment was *Victory Through Airpower* (1943), based on the controversial best-selling book by Major Alexander de Seversky, which advocated using long-range bombing against Germany and Japan. I believe that picture was as big a challenge to animate as *Fantasia,* because it meant taking a straight, serious document and converting it into a clear, understandable visual documentary. But the results were excellent. It was the first "nuts and bolts" feature made at Disney's—meaning a lot of effects animation for bomb explosions, maps, wreckage, etc. Many of the techniques developed in *Victory* have become standard for educational films. The picture was a little late being released, since the technology of airpower kept surpassing the book's recommendations. In the end, Seversky's military theories turned out to be all wrong—which the armed forces people knew all along. But the graphics we had to invent for the film were spectacular.

||||||||||||||||||||||||

Also around this time, *Der Fuhrer's Face* (1943) was on the boards. Ollie Wallace wrote a tune whose basic structure was built around a fart, or "raspberry." It was a very funny premise, designed to be a Hitler putdown—and that it was. It did the job of boosting morale, just as "Who's Afraid of the Big Bad Wolf" had done in the Great Depression. This novelty tune was a whistlin', foot-tapping' song (to use the words of Frank Churchill) and that's the best kind. The chorus went something like this:

> *"Ven der Fuhrer says ve iss der master race,*
> *Ve Heil! Heil! right in der Fuhrer's face . . ."*

The picture was built around the song, and it turned out to be a big success and won an Oscar in 1942. And I was the director. Walt, of course, picked up the award. Prints were sent all over the world, even to Russia, which used its propaganda message to encourage their troops. I don't think it was very popular with the Nazis. In fact, we heard that Hitler burned every copy he could find. We loved that.

Ollie used to say that he wrote a lot of tunes over the years, but his two big hits were "Hindustan" in World War I and "Der Fuhrer's Face" in World War II. When war broke out, he rose to the occasion.

Ollie started his career playing piano in a whorehouse. He became one of the premier organists playing the "Mighty Wurlitzer" in a prestigious theater in Seattle, Washington, before joining the music staff at Disney.

While working on "Der Fuhrer's Face," Ollie was often visited by an old chum, Isham Jones, who had composed many popular songs, including "It Had to Be You." Ish told us about the time he'd visited Ollie in the organ basement of the theater. He'd just happened to have a bottle of rotgut with him, which he and Ollie proceeded to empty. When the buzzer went off, Ollie quickly combed his hair, arranged his tails over the bench, and started to play, yelling at Ish to punch the button that hydraulically lifted him and his Wurlitzer into the theater, playing "Land of the Sky Blue Waters" for the patrons. Ollie was all over the keyboard, belting it out for the huge crowd. Finishing with a flourish, he stood and turned toward his usually enthralled, appreciative audience for applause. But there was only one desultory clapper as Ollie took his bow. He was still in the basement, and Ish was his only audience. Ish had forgotten to push the button!

Dick Kelsey, a very fine background and story layout man, volunteered for the Marine Corps and became a major. They put him in charge of building scale models of various islands to be invaded, which were a tremendous help in strategy meetings. He was commended by General MacArthur himself for his thorough relief map of Tarawa.

||||||||||||||||||||||

Some guys just weren't cut out for the military—and John Hubley was one of these. He was a very talented guy—he did layout on *Pinocchio*—but he was an unbelievable slob. He didn't care if his shoes were laced. During the war, he was stationed at "Fort Roach," the Hal Roach studio in Culver City. Later on he made films of his own and won Academy Awards.

From 1941 to 1948, foreign distribution dropped considerably because of the war, and what there was paid off slowly. In spite of the normal amount of goofing off by the inmates, production was high during this period, with 122 short subjects and many features finished— not counting the immense output of training films during the war years. But costs were rising and the studio's money problems were, as always, "iffy" (meaning normal), so much so that Walt and Roy sent all the directors a memo on "squeezing out the profits" . . .

PURPOSE OF THIS MEMORANDUM

The purpose of this memorandum is to pull together for careful study the various factors governing the operation of Walt Disney Productions for the twenty-one-month period of Jan. 1, 1947, through Sept. 30, 1948.

An analysis of the figures for the first quarter of the current fiscal year revealed that despite the reductions in personnel and other economies accomplished in the last six months, the trend of disbursements will exceed the trend of cash receipts.

On top of this disturbing factor is the bad news from Technicolor. Changes in our release schedule caused by the delay in delivery of release prints will cost the studio approximately $1,000,000 in this period of twenty-one months.

Under these circumstances, it is imperative that some plan be agreed upon which will not only prevent the company from going further into debt, but which will make possible a reduction in the bank loans.

WHAT MUST BE DONE TO GAIN THIS OBJECTIVE

The successful operation of the plan requires on one hand a constructive attitude *toward every dollar which goes into developing, producing, and selling the scheduled pictures; and on the other hand, a hard-boiled attitude toward every dollar which isn't vital to these functions.*

The objective requires a reduction in payroll, accounts payable, payroll taxes and capital additions, effective March 1, 1947, but as can be seen from the details on costs, ample funds have been provided for the production program outlined.

In order to reach the goal set, the following managerial responsibilities must be accepted and constantly watched:

1. *The production schedule should be buttoned up and not changed.*
2. *A determined effort to bring the pictures now in production across the finish line within the figures used in the projections.*
3. *The development and refinement of stories to go into production for '49 and '50 release, to the point where there will be a minimum of uncertainty and change.*
4. *A continuing effort to improve our selling and exploitation programs to the end of increasing the gross from our films. Perhaps it will help to point up the importance of carrying out some such plan as this to know that it would only take a 10% decrease in income during this period to raise the September 30, 1948, loan balance from $2,500,000 to $3,500,000.*
5. *A thorough and consistent political job on all departmental disbursements to insure the stopping of leaks and expenditures of unnecessary (luxury) dollars. Vitally necessary to watch every non-production dollar—otherwise overhead rates will go up, with a resulting rise in total picture costs.*

WALT

This went on for several pages, with columns of numbers to illustrate the points. It's crazy to think that today's multi-billion-dollar Disney company was ever so hard up for cash.

Walt always admired the top animators' talent because that was something he could never do. In the late forties he designated a group of animators "the nine old men," namely Les Clark, Marc Davis, Ollie Johnston, Milt Kahl, Ward Kimball, Eric Larson, John Lounsbery, Woolie Reitherman, and Frank Thomas. These men became Walt's board of advisers, and he listened to their opinions on many subjects.

Not included in this group, who contributed *so* much and deserved special tribute too, were Ed Aardal, Art Babbitt, Phil Duncan, Norm Ferguson, Hugh Fraser, Dick Huemer, Ub Iwerks, Bill Justice, Hal King, Fred Moore, Ken Muse, John Sibley, Howard Swift, Harvey Toombs, and Bill Tytla, all wonderfully talented animators, and Jack Boyd, Joe D'Aglio, Ugo D'Orsi, Andy Engman, Dan Macmanus, Josh Meador, John McManus, and Cy Young, the great effects animators.

The idea of picking just nine animators out of the many excellent and talented individuals associated with the studio was greatly resented by those not anointed by the master's wand. It was not good for morale. Artists, in the main, can be very touchy and are wont to vent their spleen by kicking wastebaskets, griping, pouting, and in general getting plain pissed off. But this was Walt's way, keeping everyone off balance and stirred up.

CHAPTER 9

Walt

"WHO'LL I RAISE HELL WITH NEXT?"

t isn't surprising that so many characters passed through Disney's over the years. The main man, Walt himself, was a paradigm of characters.

The public's image of Walt is, of course, that of a genuis. There's no doubt that he *was* one of a kind. Walt set his goals high and expected everyone around him to do the same. To say a thing was impossible was un-Disney.

Without the help of his brother Roy, Walt might have been just one of the dreamers who are so common among those bitten by the creative urge. We all owe much to Roy's single-minded business acumen. Walt, on the other hand, was a complex person. A dreamer, but one who pursued his goals with clarity and an almost ferocious intensity.

There was a divergence of opinion about Walt among his "troops." There were those who revered him and those who saw him simply as a person, with all the faults, frailties, and talents that make us human. Most of the hired hands at least respected Walt for his dedication and drive. Also, in the early days, Walt was the one who gave them jobs when jobs were hard to find. We were all young, and so was Walt, but he was old enough to have an edge in experience, and that was what he gave us, *experience,* a chance to experiment. Animation was a new medium and there was a lot to learn, so we were all grateful for the opportunity, even if we weren't likely to get rich quick. We were kindred souls, all ambitious to become artists, cartoonists, painters—and at Disney's it was "cut the mustard or cut out." Walt was competing and he expected everyone to help him. It was an exciting challenge.

Walt demanded respect and he got it. There was no mollycoddling.

Walt went to great lengths to portray himself as a shy person, "Uncle Walt," a kindly, self-effacing farmboy from the Midwest who prided himself on the fact that he never owned a tuxedo. He was a great admirer of Will Rogers, and copied his mannerisms in public, which added to the image. He was certainly Midwestern—waspish, down to earth—but he could swear like a trooper, and he had a terrific ego.

Ub Iwerks once remarked that Walt was very intense in whatever he did. One day at lunch, Ub told us about a time when he worked for Walt in Kansas City in the twenties. There was no work at the studio, and the boys decided to play a little poker, but not Walt. He sat at his desk, seemingly busy as hell.

His curiosity aroused, Ub tip-toed over to see what Walt was doing. He was practicing his signature. Ub tip-toed back to the game. He said he knew right then that with his ego, Walt was going to make it.

THE MAD
TAPPER

Walt roamed his domain with a hard-heeled stride that, along with his distinctive cough, warned us of his arrival. He'd crash through the door, stride to a chair, sit down, and tap his fingers on the arm until one of the guys grabbed a pointer and proceeded to tell the story.

He'd usually allow the guy to finish, then all the boys would hold their breath until he started talking. We studied him the way he studied the boards. If he coughed, you knew you'd lost his attention. A slow tap meant he was just thinking, but a fast tap meant he was losing his cool. . . .

"I LIKE IT!"

f you had something good, Walt usually said he liked it right out. Then everybody could relax and get on with the meeting. Sometimes he could be very enthusiastic, and all the guys would fly high around the room and pitch in to use his suggestions for tightening the stuff up, then help move the boards into the director's room and into production.

"SHELVE IT!"

f he didn't like it, he'd want to get out before any more money was spent. He'd stomp from the room, leaving the poor guys responsible with egg on their faces.

Walt had the most athletic eyebrows I have ever seen. He had a way of giving you the evil eye, with his finger pointed at your chest, that was very intimidating. He'd punctuate his words with "y'know, y'know, y'know," until you were answering "yeah, yeah, yeah"—whether you knew what he was talking about or not. If you didn't, you'd better damn well find out.

Walt's scare tactics kept us on our toes. As I've said, he liked to play puppeteer—juggling people around, pushing, reaching. Occasionally he would pat a guy on the back; the next day he'd ignore him. In the early days he referred to "our" products; later on, it was "my" pictures. Walt had strong likes and dislikes, and he could hold a grudge forever. The sad thing about his personality was that many artists had egos of their own that often clashed with his.

Walt pronounced words his own way, and by God you'd better learn it.

Then there were the inevitable social pariahs. We had our own unfriendly list of names for them, headed by kiss-asses, or just "KA's," umbrella-holders, arm-squeezers, winkies, smilies. They were all lumped together in a category that covered a great group from all departments. Some rose to power, and that was even worse.

Don't ever get to close to Walt," was Ben Sharpsteen's sage advice. Ben practiced what he preached, and, as proof, while fallen heads littered the tarmac, Ben stayed on until he retired.

It didn't matter who you were, if you didn't see eye-to-eye with Walt, if you got too smart with him, you could kiss your job good-bye.

Norm Ferguson, who we all thought was essential to the studio, took his leave by asking Walt to leave him alone. That was the beginning of the end for him.

Ken Darby wrote a damn fine piece of music for *Johnny Appleseed*. He played it for a lot of the guys, who all liked it very much. Then he played it for Walt, who criticized it none too kindly. Ken's comeback became an in-joke that we never forgot. Of course, he never wrote again for Disney's after that, but he went on to become one of the top music men in the movie business.

It was bandied about by the boys in the back room that Walt stopped in the studio basement on his way in to change into his mood costume for the day. These moods were known as "the Seven Faces of Walt."

Once, Dick Kelsey, Jack Cutting, and I were interviewed about Walt. The reporter asked us to describe his sense of humor. Jack Cutting thought about it for a minute, then came up with just the right answer. The sorts of things that tickled Walt were outhouse gags, goosing gags, bedpans and johnny pots, thinly disguised farts, and cows' udders.

Some of the old hands said that Walt mellowed as Disney's income soared into astronomical figures with the parks, TV programs, and merchandising programs all in operation. When he died, things became unglued—there was no guiding light. The studio tried to run its operations by committee since no one had been groomed to take his place. With the studio rudderless, the product declined. Only the magic name of Disney kept it afloat.

CHAPTER 10

The Evils of Drink

All work and no play makes Jack a dull boy, to quote the well-known adage.

From bootleg beer in Prohibition days to martinis—drinking was the inmates' prevalent habit. Of course, Walt was no exception. When we worked late, we often saw his car swerve out of the parking lot as he headed home to Westwood. That was quite a long way to go, but he always made it. He must have had someone watching over him.

For most of us, weekends were the time for socializing. But come Monday, all the elves left the real world and returned to the land of fantasy—nursing hangovers. Mouth tasting like the inside of a motorman's glove, head in a vise, nerves unglued, eyes feeling like sandpaper, body aching, stomach churning, hair hurting . . . sometimes we wondered if it was worth it.

‖‖‖‖‖‖‖‖‖‖‖‖‖‖‖‖‖‖‖

John Sibley stopped for a quick one with the boys once while on his way home from work—and you know how it is with convivial companions. Later (much later) John arrived home only to find his loving wife, Jane, waiting up for him. She was dressed in her best finery—furs, hat, gloves, jewels. Then it occurred to John that he had promised to take her dining and dancing to celebrate their wedding anniversary.

John, ever able to cope with any situation, blithely asked "What's new?" Naturally, Jane saw the humor of this and forgave him his oversight—three years later.

TICK TOCK

Queen of the martini set," Retta Scott was the first woman animator at Disney's and a truly fine artist. She did animation on *Bambi*. Rumor had it that she had two hollow legs. The truth was, she could drink anyone under the table, and she did. The next day she'd be fresh as a daisy. For her drinking companions, the next day's awakening was known as the "Dread Scott Decision."

A lot of pilots who flew out of Burbank lived in my neighborhood. Talk about characters—these boys made some of our Disney inmates seem sedate by comparison. Captain Charles Francis Sullivan of United Air Lines lived across the street, and soon I met lots more crazy, wonderful people. We'd play tennis at the abandoned Sunset Canyon Country Club, swim in Sulley's pool, then drink—oh, how we would drink.

After one lost weekend, I departed for the studio at eight on Monday morning while the flyboys slept it off. It was a beautiful day—sun up, no clouds (we didn't have smog in those days), blue skies—bright and gorgeous. Only I didn't feel either bright or gorgeous. At 8:30 A.M. I lowered myself into my chair, holding what was left of my head, when I was startled by the jangling of the phone. It was Dolores, Walt's secretary: "Hello, Jack, Walt wants you up in his office right away." "Okay," I said, gingerly replacing the receiver in its cradle.

Pulling myself together, I mounted the stairs feeling like Marie Antoinette on her way to the guillotine.

Walt was in fine fettle, leaning back in his chair, silhouetted against the venetian blinds. He told me to have a seat, and I groped my way to his "settee," which was a very uncomfortable, straight-backed, hard-packed bit of furniture fronted by a glass-topped table. Walt was in a talkative mood, wanting to discuss *Peter Pan,* to which I had been assigned.

"Y'want some coffee?" he asked.

Of course I wanted some coffee, and I also wanted and needed about eighteen hours of sleep. Dolores poured coffee into a cup on a saucer with a spoon and graciously set it in front of me on the glass table.

Walt started in, and I was all ears, trying to pay attention and enjoy his enthusiasm. Surreptitiously, I reached for the nectar of the gods. I had the *shakes.* I was trying to sneak up and grasp the rim of the saucer and escort it to my grieving lips—when all hell broke loose. The sound effects of saucer, cup, and spoon on the table were awesome. I tried to

cope, while looking toward the variegated image of a man intent on discussing the intricate process of putting a several-million-dollar picture into
production. But in reality, I couldn't cope with getting that gawdamned cup
up to my lips.

Walt wasn't about to let me off easy. That particular early-morning in-
quisition went on till about noon.

Almost every day there'd be a couple of noontime late entries, back from Alphonse's. Bill Peet and Ralph Wright were buddies. Ted Sears used to say Ralph "walked with the wind" and Bill "walked against the wind."

If Frank Churchill came back from lunch feeling for the banisters . . . and walking on eggshells . . . he had a snootful.

CRUNCH

CRUNCH

On one occasion, Sue Bristol, head of the Ink and Paint Department, came home from a date with Frank Oreb, a very handsome and talented artist. Sue had quite a temper. She thought she'd locked herself out, and threw her shoe through a big plate-glass window. It turned out the door wasn't locked after all.

One morning, Dick Shaw, another great gag man, stopped to pick up Dick Kinney for work—and woke him up. Dick and his date had been drinking and swimming the night before, after which my exhausted brother had fallen asleep. His neglected date had penned her revenge in lipstick on his tummy.

Dick Shaw didn't like to carry much cash. He was quite generous, however, and often bought drinks for others. Sorting out his bar tabs each month became known as "the day of reckoning."

Sometimes the boys and girls had no choice but to sleep it off. Each person had his or her favorite spot.

Our angel of mercy was Hazel George, R.N., who dispensed enormous amounts of pink pills that we believed to be a sure cure for anything from hangovers to ague, anxiety, sprains, spasms, pip, gout, athlete's foot, acne, and hangnails. They were truly a miracle potion, dispensed from "Witch Hazel" with love.

A lot of the guys lived down in Balboa, and they'd have parties on weekends. Tom Adair's bar saw plenty of action. Tom was a real sweetheart of a guy, and he wrote awfully good song lyrics . . . but his wife ran the show.

We worked together, we played together, and we drank together. For most of us, producing gags and coming up with funny situations and comical happenings was a daily necessity and never far below the conscious level in our minds. Maybe more ideas were quenched than born in our frequent forays to favorite bars for liquid inspiration. But somehow the next day we'd pour out new ideas like the bartender had poured drinks the night before.

CHAPTER

11

Latter Days

From the time I first thought of leaving the Disney organization in 1945 until I was ungainfully employed in 1957, I had the uncomfortable feeling that my time in the Mouse Factory was coming to a close.

For several months, Tex Avery, director of MGM's cartoon division, had been telling me that Fred Quimby, head of the Shorts Department, wanted to talk to me about leaving Disney's. Finally, Tex called one day and said that Mr. Quimby wanted to meet with me the following Saturday. Well, why not?

Saturday morning I met with Quimby. He sat, as Walt used to, with his back to the window, so that bright light would filter through the slats of his venetian blinds and into my eyes. He got right to the point and asked what I was making at Disney's.

"Two hundred per week, which is really one hundred seventy because of a fifteen-percent hold-off cut, to be paid later," I said. (It never was, of course.)

"Well," Quimby said, "I'll pay you three hundred fifty for the first year, and then five hundred for the second year, and seven hundred fifty after that."

I thought that rather nice, but told him that I had a contract at Disney's and didn't know if I could break it. "However," I added, "Walt doesn't usually stand in the way if somebody really wants out."

He asked me to let him know as soon as possible, because he wanted to start another unit (besides Tex Avery's and Hanna and Barbera's). We shook hands and I left after a tour of the studio.

The following Monday morning I called Walt's office and asked if I could see him. With bated breath I told him of Quimby's offer. He nodded, then started finger-drumming on the arm of his chair.

After a long spell he said, "Well, you've got a contract with me, and I won't let you go."

"No?" I said.

"No, but I'll meet Quimby's offer." And he did.

Shortly after that, I got a new contract as a producer-director.

Once again Walt called me to his office. "I've been thinking of starting up again on *Peter Pan*," he said. (*Peter Pan* had been on the shelf for about ten years.) "Now here's what I want you to do. I want you to move into 2F and we'll knock a connecting door into the large room across from the library, and you can use it as a story conference room where you can hang your boards. Then I want you to go full blast into production."

I picked a basic crew that included some top talents, and we moved in with our desks, personal belongings, and Eliot Daniel's piano. It was a gung-ho bunch. Then Walt said he wanted us to try a new approach. "Take each sequence one at a time; develop it and script it. Then, when each written sequence is approved, on to the next one, and so on until we have a completed script from start to finish. We'll have a story meeting every morning on the written material being developed, then into production. Also, I want two nights of overtime as well as Saturday—okay?"

"Okay," I said.

"Get started. We want to get the damn thing out!"

We all pitched in. Each morning we delivered the following day's script to Walt so he could take it home and read it. Soon sequences were being okayed, and we started storyboarding, setting the characters, and auditioning the voices at night with the help of talent scout Jack Rourke.

Meanwhile, Eliot Daniel was banging out some great tunes. Everything was moving along very well. All the men and women in the unit were enthusiastic. The storyboards and model sheets were taking shape.

From time to time I would run into Walt and he'd ask, "How's it going?" I'd always say, "Fine," and then, "Wouldn't you like to see what's done, because there are a few spots we'd like to change."

"No," he'd say, "I don't want to see it until it's finished, and don't change anything in the script."

"Okay," I'd say, and we'd go along as we were.

Finally, after about six months, all the boards were completed, thirty-nine of them, four by eight feet. Each board carried more than one hundred sketches, totaling close to 400,000 sketches, all rendered in pastel, with the dialogue, action, and sound effects pasted underneath, representing a tremendous number of man-hours.

Now we were ready to display our handiwork. About twenty people were invited, including Walt, for this premiere. The troops assembled and I began selling the material to the jaundiced audience.

It was a two-and-a-half-hour concentrated performance, with no interruptions from the assembled group. At the end I leaned on the last storyboard, completely pooped, my mouth dry, gasping for breath.

There was a long pause. The only sound was that of Walt's tapping fingers as everyone waited for the man's first reaction. Finally his mind was made up. With a final accent on the arm of his chair, he announced, "Y'know, I've been thinking of Cinderella."

At that, the whole gathering of kiss-asses came alive—"Yeah, Walt"; "Yeah, great idea"; "Cute, timeless"; "A love story"; "A classic"—with assorted giggles, outright laughs, and knee-slapping. I couldn't believe it!

Since I was near the door, I quietly left the room and headed for Alfonse's for a couple of slugs and a bit of sustenance. I was soon joined by a few of our group with the same idea.

The picture was shelved and, as far as we knew, so was the unit and the dream. On returning from lunch we all had a proper "wake." (*Peter Pan* was finally released in 1953.)

IIIIIIIIIIIIIIIIIIIIIIIIII

The unit was ignored for a while, then we were assigned to a thing that had been around for almost as long as *Peter Pan*—*Bongo,* a short story by Sinclair Lewis based on a circus bear. So it was off the shelf and into our laps. It was a dog. You have to work twice as hard on a story of that kind . . . and we tried. Eliot Daniel wrote some good tunes for it, and Dinah Shore was cast as the narrator. Dinah was a pleasure to work with, and we ended up with a good sound track. That always helps. It was impossible to stretch the story to a full-length feature, so another dog came off the shelf—*The Mickey Feature*. Bill Roberts directed this section. A young singer did the songs, and at last the two were released as *Fun and Fancy Free* (1947).

Next we made a few Goofy shorts. Then we caught another shelved feature, *The Wind in the Willows.* We used what we could, and added a chase and a few other things to it. Then I co-directed with Gerry Geronimi on *Ichabod Crane,* with Bing Crosby singing and narrating—another enjoyable experience. These two pictures were released as *The Adventures of Ichabod and Mr. Toad* (1949), and that was the last feature I worked on at Disney's.

‖‖‖‖‖‖‖‖‖‖‖‖‖‖‖‖‖‖‖

Once again, it was back to shorts. Then came television and Disneyland. I was one of the first assigned to television development. And my first job? Figure out a way to introduce Walt on the show. He made it perfectly clear that he expected me to find some gimmick. It had to be a comfortable arrangement that didn't require much acting on his part. "Because," he said, "I'm not much of an actor, y'know. Maybe some kind of narrator or something. One thing for sure, I don't want to be behind a desk in a library. That's out! If there's anything I can't stand, it's someone behind a desk in a library, pontificating on his supposed knowledge. Is that clear?"

"Yeah," I said, "that's clear."

So I threw ideas around. There were a lot of areas to explore, and I tried them all: animation rooms, music rooms, Camera Department, Cutting and Editing, sound stages, Ink and Paint, Special Effects, Background Department, and even the mail room, to name just a few.

What did he end up doing? Sitting in a library behind a desk. Oh, well. We tried.

Soon we started going through the old pictures, trying to find an excuse to tie them together with some kind of continuity for television. We skimmed the cream off the top, putting four or five shorts into a package and making it look like original material. (You only had to fill out forty-eight minutes, because the balance of the hour was taken up by commercials and trailers for next week's show.) And then, soon enough, we were scraping the bottom of the barrel. It was dog work. The creative fun was gone.

175

The grand opening of Disneyland in 1955 followed a big tub-thumping campaign in the news media, especially on TV. The studio personnel and their families were all invited as window dressing—as were celebrities and the press, with, of course, the whole shebang on television. It was a very hot Sunday, and the whole thing was disorganized except for the live television coverage. All of the loyal employees were assigned various areas to populate, such places as Tomorrowland, Fantasyland, Frontierland, and Adventureland.

We were allowed to case the joint until two o'clock, when we had to report to our various stations. My group was assigned to the Mark Twain Riverboat. We gaily tripped up the plank and wandered around. It was still hot, and the passengers were all sweating on the crowded boat. There was no bar, fountain, or water aboard, and no way to jump ship after you were on. Some so-and-so had removed the gangplank!

We were ready to mutiny when at last Art Linkletter and Walt came aboard. The television cameras and crew moved in, and we were all on live television, waving happily at the cameras as the whistle tootled, bells rang, and fake smoke issued from the stacks. Walt and Art Linkletter and the television crews moved on, and so did the crew as the gangplank was lowered. Like rats deserting a sinking ship, we pushed and shoved to reach dry land, drank warm colas at the Frontierland Saloon, and escaped in our cars to the nearest bars, and then home after a memorable day.

Later we traded stories with other employees and found that some were locked in cattle cars on the Disneyland railroad, marooned on Tom Sawyer's Island, restricted to the crowded theater, and jammed into rocket rides and other "fun" places. But at least we could all say we were there.

stayed in Story, trying to develop material. About this time, the ABC brass wanted to see what was cooking. I had developed a six-hour program called *The History of Aviation,* going from Icarus to outer space. We'd done plenty of research, with tremendous support from the entire aviation industry, including the Archives of Aviation, the FAA, Lockheed, and McDonnell-Douglas. It was a beautiful undertaking, including all the old films, stories, and personalities from the Montgolfiers to the Wright brothers and beyond. I was amazed at all the glamour, heartbreak, and breakthroughs in the stories of these pioneers.

When we presented the material to ABC, we got what amounted to a standing ovation. Even Walt was impressed, and the picture was rushed quickly into production.

Then, lo and behold, an ultimatum was handed down. An animator who had just been promoted to director was assigned to "Man in Space," while I was left "holding the bag" with the history section. Walt was so intrigued with the space material that he gave it preference. Without much of a buildup, I was "painted into a corner" (an old Disney expression) with no place to go. That's when I knew my Disney days were numbered. The gravy was flowing the other way. Of course, I had suspected since the Tex Avery–MGM affair, with subsequent clues, that I had made a boo-boo. It seems that my raise had somehow leaked out and Walt was forced to give equal pay to all of the directors. Walt didn't like to be forced into anything and he had an unforgiving memory, so the handwriting was on the wall, and those carrots he had tossed my way were long gone.

It was soon clear that others knew of my situation. The kiss-asses ignored me. Ostracism set in. I was shunned by erstwhile "friends," I was a leper, shunted about, shied away from, and off limits—a rat among the mice.

I felt kind of alone, but then I got my first fan letter.

Pound Rd. *June 11, 1957*
Dist. #6
Westerly, Rhode Island

Dear Mr. Kinney,

I have seen your name on many of Walt Disney's productions, one for instance is the motion picture Pinocchio. On the Mickey Mouse Club I have often seen your name also. Mr. Kinney I can't think of what you do, produce, direct or what, so Sir I would appreciate it very much if you would answer this letter. You see my name is "Jack Kinney" also! If you do answer this letter would you please tell me what you do for Mr. Disney, if you are married, would you please give me your autograph and if it is possibly could you get me Mr. Disney's autograph. I would appreciate it very much.

Mr. Kinney did you have anything to do with the picture "Johnny Tremain"? That should be a very good picture.

I am 13 years of age (going on 15 I mean 14 the 25 of June) I am in the 8th grade.

Yours truly,
(signed)
Jack Kinney

P.S.   I have two horses.

Before long, the ax fell. One of the middle-management guys gave me a call and said, "Can I see you in private?" I said, "Naw, I know what it's all about. When can I leave?" Aghast that he wouldn't have a chance to give me the news, he stuttered, "Well . . . uh . . . anytime, but you know you've got two weeks' severance pay coming."

"Fine," I said, "I'll just pack a few personal belongings and be off." Which I did, after writing a short interoffice memo to Walt (who, naturally, was out of town). It merely said, "On February 9, 1931, you told me I could have a job, but it might be only temporary. I believed you then and I know it now. Thanks for keeping me out of pool halls this long. Jack."

Was there life after Disney? I was about to find out in the year A.D. 1957.

It wasn't until I had ventured outside the six-foot chain-link fence that "protected" the studio grounds that I really understood the meaning of the Disney roller-coaster syndrome.

By the time I departed, the tracks were straightening out and the curves weren't as sharp. But I soon learned to appreciate what Walt and Roy had had to go through before that smooth ride was possible.

Some were able to hold on, with stock options and other niceties. In the meantime, like many other Disney alumni, I had to bite and scratch and clamber. It was a new world. We had to ring doorbells, make contacts, meet people, and try to get a foot in the door, all the while coping with the popular view that animation was prohibitively costly. Only a few studios were doing theatrical animated films. Television was in; animated commercials were in; the advertising agencies were tin gods. It was exciting and tough. "Think cheap" was the motto in the cartoon game.

I'd been on the beach for about two weeks when I got a mysterious phone call from Harry Tytle, who was in upper management at Disney's.

"Can you meet me for lunch at Musso and Frank's?" he asked.

"Okay," I said.

When I arrived, Hal Adelquist was there, too. Hal had been out in the new world for about a year and claimed to have "connections." Hal had also been very close to Walt. In fact, he was sometimes known as a "whipping boy" or "umbrella holder." He was always cheerful and enthusiastic, no matter what lousy job he had to carry out—although he did have a nervous tic and the shakes. At various times he was in casting; he'd been the business unit head of the Story Department, and finally the associate producer of "The Mickey Mouse Club." Then he fell from grace. Some blamed it on a dread concoction known as vodka. He had hail-fellowed and well-met a few too many times.

Harry slid into the booth, beaming. "Walt asked me to ask you if you would be interested in doing an hour Disney program on the outside starring Goofy. There's only once clause . . . "

"Yeah, yeah?" we both answered.

". . . that you two form a production company."

"A production company?" we echoed. "How do you do that?" "Easy," said Harry. "Just open up shop. Call it Adelquist-Kinney or Kinney-Adelquist, whichever."

We mulled this over. The initials A&K or K&A translated to "asskissing" or "kiss-assing," neither of which had much stature in the industry lexicon. We hoped this wouldn't catch on as we flipped a coin. I won, and thus the great company of Kinney-Adelquist Productions, Inc., was formed.

How mercurial! From a lowly, unemployed doorbell ringer to the president of an organization that was sure to make its presence felt in the world of entertainment. What with Hal and his contacts and my wife, Jane (also an alumnus of the Disney empire), as secretary-treasurer, we had it made. We had a bona fide contract from Walt Disney himself—a prestigious assignment to produce a full-hour television show on a national television network, with, we naturally hoped, more to follow. We were on our way. Or so we thought.

We set up shop on Highland Avenue, across from Hollywood High School. Hollywood, the movie capital of the world! A far cry from Burbank, a hick town founded by a dentist in 1878. Anyway, we were open for business and we got it. The subject we were doing for Walt was *Water, Water Everywhere*. Our storyboards were turning out just fine—good gags, good sequences, a natural for Goofy. Little did I know that Hal kept Walt advised on just how good it was—not once, but over and over, and always late at night and under the influence of vodka.

In the meantime, Phil Duncan, a fine animator, continued putting the boards together. We had many drop-ins and managed to pick up some smaller jobs as well. Finally the boards were finished and Walt was so informed by Hal and was asked to come in for a story meeting. Time went by, but Walt didn't show. Hal became more insistent. Phil and I started working on other material.

At last we got a phone call from the studio, and a meeting was set for the following day, but not with Walt. Instead he sent over an assortment of people who obviously had orders to turn the picture down, and they did. Our "Water" was cut off. The storyboards were picked up by a studio truck the next day, and so *Water, Water Everywhere* went nowhere. The roller coaster headed down.

Much later, our picture was made as *Water Mania* by the studio. That was that.

Luckily we had other things to work on—religious films, a few commercials, a pilot for *Li'l Pedro,* based on Bill de la Torres's comic strip for the Dell Publishing Company. During this period Hal had been living with Jane and me "temporarily." Finally, after several months, we insisted he find other lodgings. He did, and we regained our home and especially our bar.

About this time we began a new venture, Puerto Rico. While at Disney's I became friendly with a man sent by the Puerto Rican government to the Disney studio to find out how animation could be used to teach the undereducated outlying people of the hills. His name was Val Torres, or Don Valentin Torres-Valdez. Val was the Minister of Education and connected with WIPR, the Puerto Rican government's educational TV station. He was a complete aficionado of animation, enthusiastic, knowledgeable, soft-spoken, and pleasant. Val spent several weeks at the studio, and I was lucky enough to be assigned to him.

Later, Val urged me to come to Puerto Rico and open a studio there.

Leaving Hal Adelquist in charge of Kinney-Adelquist, we took off. Puerto Rico had a lot to offer: there was no competition from other animation studios; the move would be tax-free for ten years, with government financing for land, buildings, and studio facilities; the climate was wonderful, and the people friendly and cooperative. By the time we left, I was sold on the idea.

At the New York airport on the way back, I was minding my own business when some guy came up behind me and slapped me on the back. It was Walt. "Where have you been?" he asked.

"Puerto Rico," I said. Then I told him of our plans. He was interested and offered a bit of kind advice: "Keep a sharp pencil with you all the time." Just then there was an announcement over the PA. Walt's wife, Lily, rushed up to him. "Walt, I've been looking all over for you. Hurry, we have to get aboard." Walt hesitated, and turning back to me, he said, "Y'know, I'm sorry about that TV show, but y'know I just can't be pushed into something like that by anybody. You know who I mean."

"Forget it," I said. That was the last time I ever talked to "himself."

Upon returning to the Coast, we kept the Puerto Rican project on the fire, discussing it with various financial people as well as lining up talent who would be willing to pull up stakes and work in Puerto Rico. No problem. Almost everyone wanted to get on to this gravy train in the sky.

Conditions at Kinney-Adelquist were mighty shaky. Hal had kind of disappeared. I was wondering what to do next when Steve Bosustow at UPA called. He wanted me to direct Mr. Magoo's first feature, *1001 Arabian Nights* (1959). I agreed to help out on a temporary basis, because I had high hopes for Puerto Rico. This was okay with Steve.

Considerable work had already been done on the feature, but it was a mess. However, it was a fine experience for me, because it meant I had

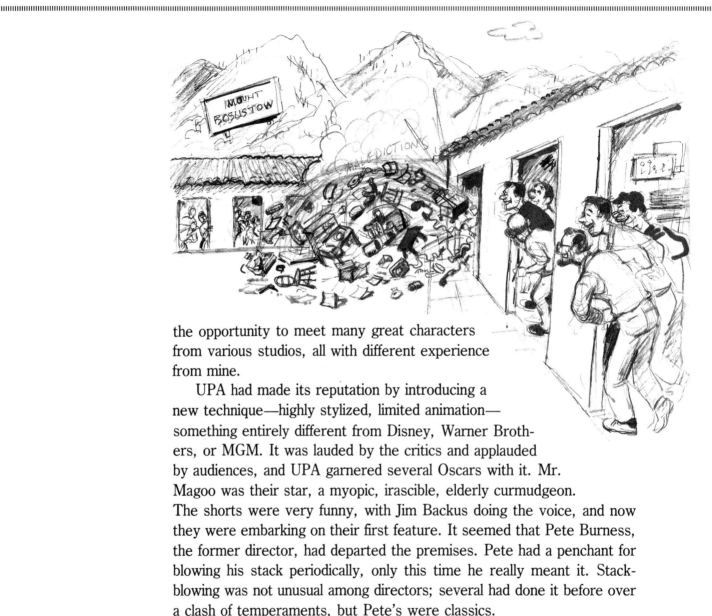

the opportunity to meet many great characters from various studios, all with different experience from mine.

UPA had made its reputation by introducing a new technique—highly stylized, limited animation—something entirely different from Disney, Warner Brothers, or MGM. It was lauded by the critics and applauded by audiences, and UPA garnered several Oscars with it. Mr. Magoo was their star, a myopic, irascible, elderly curmudgeon. The shorts were very funny, with Jim Backus doing the voice, and now they were embarking on their first feature. It seemed that Pete Burness, the former director, had departed the premises. Pete had a penchant for blowing his stack periodically, only this time he really meant it. Stack-blowing was not unusual among directors; several had done it before over a clash of temperaments, but Pete's were classics.

The picture had a very skimpy budget, but opportunely other studios were cutting back on staff, so a steady trickle of animators, story men, and layout and background guys were thrown out into the empty animation world. I was able to pick up some very good talent.

While at UPA, I was able to keep in touch with potential clients for my own company, one of them being Al Brodax of King Features. They were about to launch a new series for Popeye on TV, and I soon signed a contract for more than one hundred of the little five-minute darlings.

I set up shop on a crash program. Of the many talented people available, quite a few who joined us were ex-Disney, including animators Harvey Toombs, Hugh Fraser, Ken Hultgren, Rudy Larriva, Cal Howard, and Grace Stanzell; story men Ed Nofziger, Al Bertino, and Dick Kinney; and Evie Sherwood and Juanita McClurg, both excellent checkers. We used various services for ink and paint, inbetween camera, cutting, and so on, and started cranking out Popeyes by the dozen for a very reasonable sum. Ken Lowman wrote original music for each, and my son Mike came into the act as a film editor and cameraman. We had a hard-working group and really knocked 'em out on schedule. Our theme song was, "I'm lookin' at the world through green-colored glasses—everything is spinach now." In addition to the Popeyes, we were doing pilots on *Krazy Kat* and *Barney Google* with our own crew. But alas, the Popeye series was eventually taken to Italy because it could be done cheaper there than in the United States.

Once again it was time to scramble for new product. One of the most common afflictions of everyone ever bitten by the cartoon bug is to hit a winner, a cartoon strip, magazine illustrations and gags, commercials, a continuing series, a feature, maybe a lot of features—something *great*. But it ain't that easy. Lots of ideas and dreams of glory . . . but mostly for the fun of it.

After the Popeye series was completed, I set up shop on Cahuenga Boulevard in North Hollywood. Cahuenga Boulevard was known as "Animation Alley" at that time. Hanna-Barbera was building a huge new studio across the street. Ray Patin's studio was four doors down, Les Novros's next door. Nearby were Gus Jekel's Film Fair, Chuck Couch Productions, Filmation, Foto-Kem Lab, Chuck Hawes Camera and Cutting Service, and Marion O'Callahan's Ink and Paint Services. Even the Screen Cartoonists Guild Union was there, all between Barham Boulevard and Laurel Canyon. The age of limited animation had begun in full force.

UPA had started it, and Hanna-Barbera, out of necessity, had adapted their style to the new medium. Television had done away with theatrical short subjects. The old-line studios had priced themselves out of the animation business. This new wave had opened a door to all of the talented people dumped into the streets. It was a blessing at the time. Animators who had been doing ten and twenty feet per week now had to turn out fifty and a hundred feet to get a job. Half-hour shows cost less than a five-minute theatrical cartoon. Only advertising clients could afford the cost of full animation. The prima donnas had to produce footage or get lost. Pencil tests were a thing of the past. Steady employment, forget it. Animation was a seasonal occupation. Some of the boys and girls quickly adapted. Others changed their careers.

||||||||||||||||||||||||||||

For the most part, animation people were living in a fantasy world, dreamers who had a thousand and one ideas that could have been turned into practical, profitable income. But it wasn't to be. Many good stories have gone begging simply because they never got off the drawing board. The big reason for this is, of course, that their creators misspent their youths trying to perfect their craft. Very few had any bent for the hard facts of business or finance. Money was something that came to them in a weekly paycheck (sometimes). So most of their ideas were just that, "hoovering" (as Walt used to say) around in their minds, while hot-air balloonists sometimes got their baskets off the ground.

True, there are exceptions. Hanna-Barbera, Chuck Jones, David DePatie, Friz Freleng, Dick Williams, Ralph Bakshi, Bill Melendez, and UPA come to mind. Many more were successful in producing commercials, educationals, strip films, documentaries, comics, and industrials. And others went into service—ink and paint, cutting, Xerox, camera.

I know I also played the dreamer many times. I call it part of growing up. But how long does it take to reach adulthood? Nobody really knows.

I tried, with my limited business abilities. Sometimes I thought I was on the brink. I had the ideas and was beginning to make contacts.

I had a friend, Fenton Earnshaw, a writer and at the time producer of "77 Sunset Strip," a TV show out of Warner Brothers. Fenton's father had originated "Chandu the Magician," a popular radio show that lasted more than twenty years. I called Fenton, and he thought reviving the show for TV was a great idea. Not only that, but he and his brother had saved every one of his father's scripts, hundreds of them.

So Hugh Fraser and I started developing storyboards for animation. Our hopes were high and so were MCA's, except at that time MCA was backing another property, based on "Amos 'n' Andy," called "Calvin and the Colonel." It bombed, went over budget, and had to be bailed out by MCA, who had just bought Universal.

That quickly dampened MCA's desire to be part of another revival, and so we had to say good-bye to Chandu, and to the two thousand dollars we had paid to the Earnshaws for rights.

||||||||||||||||||||||||

Next, an agent who represented Mae West asked if we would like to do a series on her, titled "Pretty Mae" "You damn well betcha," was our reply. So we had story meetings with her at our studio, and even dropped in to see her in her penthouse atop her Ravenswood apartments, in her white-and-gold bedroom complete with circular bed, mirrored ceiling, and pet spider monkeys. She was indeed a real lady. She believed in proper diet, exercise, and no booze or tobacco. She had a delightful personality and a great gag and story sense, very clean dialogue and speech, only innuendo, a real pleasure to work with.

But, alas, as happens so often in Hollywood, a contract couldn't be negotiated and the deal fell through.

WHAT CAN I DO?

Then Bill Dana landed at our door. He was a very talented guy, a writer, producer, gag man, actor, comedian, author, publisher—you name it, Bill had done it. Except an animated cartoon. So he and I got together and made a pilot based on "Jose Jimenez," a very successful character he had created and recorded. It was warm, friendly, and funny, and ideally suited for a series. But even in those days, ethnic characterizations had a few trapdoors, and our nice little series fell through one of them.

Our next thrilling adventure came when we were approached by W. C. Fields's family agent, Ron Leaf, representing Fields's son, W. C. Fields, Jr., a prominent attorney who looked like his father and could do his voice to perfection. He was a marvelous man who neither drank nor smoked, explaining that his mother had asked him not to until he was twenty years old. He had honored his mother's wishes, and by the time he reached twenty, he had no desire to try. We thought we had a winner. He was writing a book and had collected all of his father's memorabilia. So again we got enthused, doing story treatments and model sheets. And again came complications. We had to abandon the project, another near miss.

About that time, Mitch Hamilburg came along with an idea for a book he represented, *Your Rugged Constitution*, based on the United States Constitution. Published by Stanford University Press, it was in its thirteenth printing. Mitch offered to handle a large part of the financing if we would donate our time on spec. Of course we would, and so there we went again. Oddly, when I was still at Disney's, Walt had brought me the same book and asked me to read it and develop it into a "Disneyland" show. I did read it and was very much in favor of doing it. But in about three weeks, when I was just getting up steam, Walt called and said grumpily, "Forget it." No reason, just forget it. I did.

Several years later I mentioned this to Mitch, and also to Bruce and Esther Finley, who had written the book. Bruce immediately said, "I remember it well. Essentially, Walt wanted to steal it from us, and I said positively 'No.'" This, apparently, had been the reason for the scratch.

The story amused both Mitch and the Finleys, who became more enthusiastic about the production. Both Hugh Fraser and I worked our tails off developing the storyboards. We all felt sure that this subject would be a shoo-in because so few people in the whole United States knew what the Constitution was all about. We felt it could be one of a whole series on patriotic subjects if they were made entertaining as well as educational, and we knew we could accomplish this.

We contacted Tom Blackburn, another old friend who was and is a damn fine writer. Tom had written *Davy Crockett*, including the song lyrics, for Disney. He was ecstatic, so with his help we put together a short subject called *The Declaration of Independence*. Now we had a package, with more to follow.

Unfortunately, Mitch Hamilburg died and so did this project. To make a long story short, we had interest from several sources, but not enough to come up with the considerable sum needed for production.

About this time we moved again, to a studio with a large stage on McCadden Place in Hollywood, but times were tough.

Then it looked as if we had caught a brass ring on the merry-go-round. Elwyn Ambrose dropped in. Elwyn was a wonderfully fey Welshman. Rex Harrison at 20th Century-Fox had brought him over to do puppetry for *Doctor Dolittle*. While there, he proposed a combination live-action and animation feature starring a friend, Marcel Marceau, the great French mime, and using the drawing style of Saul Steinberg. It was okayed by the Fox brass. A budget was set for a one-minute test. Marcel Marceau's stand-in acted in the part, and Academy Award winners Bill Abbott and Art Cruickshank did the special effects. It was first-cabin all the way, with a full crew and a large stage, and the results were wonderful. Everyone was happy with it. All systems were go. Except for one small item: Elwyn had not gotten Steinberg's final consent. The production was canceled. What next?

Next was a sudden climb. A company called Computer Sciences wanted us to do a half-hour indoctrination show on the computer and thousands of slides for their program. It was a very ambitious undertaking, but properly financed, and it was to be a continuing situation. We started making money.

Things looked good. We hired a large staff and started cranking things out. They were all good people, but when our work for Computer Sciences was finished, I'd had enough of running a business employing a lot of staff. I decided there was only one thing to do: start all over again. No more trying to keep talented people working by pounding the pavement looking for jobs. No more worrying about health and welfare, union dues, state, city, county, and federal taxes, sales taxes, use taxes—and more taxes—and not counting overhead. Forget it. I set up a studio at home—a one-man studio. Let somebody else worry about the bookkeeping. I was a free man.

Free! Free! Except I wasn't making any money. It was time to get out of the car or pay the price for another ride.

I'd been riding for almost ten years—since leaving Disney's—so I looked around and started writing comic books. It was a drag, but it was possible to make some kind of living. Then—ding-a-ling—"Can you come down and talk about a new series?" It was Ira Englander, a man we had done many hospital training films for. "I've been trying to get in touch with you for some time. Can you meet me and the Sherman brothers tomorrow night at their office?"

"Uh-huh," I said, as I jotted down the address.

That was how it started all over again, only this time somebody else was minding the store. This time it was fun. I was back creating again. Dick and Bob Sherman, Ira Englander, and me. The company was Musiclassics and the subject was *The Adventures of Sir Puss-in-Boots,* a full-length feature, with music written by the Sherman brothers, Academy Award–winning songwriters for *Mary Poppins*.

After all the many wrong turns and a few right ones, I had found a spot where I could communicate with a bunch of nice guys. Sammy Davis, Jr., Karl Malden, Michael Jackson, and others supplied the talent, singing and dancing and romancing. It was great, putting together a funny, tuneful animated cartoon fit for family entertainment.

We had a small but efficient crew who were banging the stuff out. Everything was pose-tested until we had the final eighty-two minutes fully assembled, with about twenty minutes finished in color for the key sequences. Now we were ready to show it to prospective buyers. It was screened for Frank Yablans of Paramount Pictures, and he liked it. We waited for the contract, but when we finally saw it, alas, it had many items in it that had not been agreed on. The picture was shelved, and we were left sitting on eighty-two minutes of blood, sweat, and tears. However, we still have that eighty-two minutes in the can and will continue to look elsewhere for a few hundred thousand to finish the picture.

The roller coaster was down again, and so was I. But then Ira Englander asked me to join his company, Comprenetics, as art director and head of animation—all was not lost.

With all their seriousness, the people at Comprenetics were a crazy bunch. Tom Kennington was the leader. He'd been a reporter with Hearst, and had a wealth of experience in all forms of show business. Tom kept things loose with his droll sense of humor.

I was involved in several good projects there over the next decade or so, but one of the most interesting was teaching the Navajo Indians animation. We opened our act at Fort Wingate High School in Gallup, New Mexico, with an art contest to find twenty-five Navajo high school kids with a flair for drawing. Picking twenty-five out of the several hundred entries wasn't easy. Those kids had a natural feel for animation, color, and design. Within two weeks, our group had them doing personal tests, backgrounds, ink and paint, and character development.

We shot all the kids' tests and showed them to the Navajo Tribal Council and the Bureau of Indian Affairs. They were enthusiastic, and we were okayed to continue the program. At the end of two semesters, the Navajo boys and girls, aged fourteen to eighteen, had completed a full ten-minute short picture based on a Navajo legend. This was an amazing accomplishment, and we were all higher than kites over the results.

We began designing storyboards and material for a continual flow of products that would enable the students to learn a trade that would be a lifetime occupation.

During our first seminar with the Navajo students, we had shown a group of Disney pictures, and each had the usual "Walt Disney Presents" on the opening title. After watching all these pictures, one boy from Tuba City asked me, "Say, Jack, who is Walt Disney?"

At first I thought he was kidding, then I realized he was sincere. I tried to explain. "Well, he was a producer."

"What's a producer?"

"Well, you know, he paid our salaries."

"Oh!" said the boy. "What else?"

"He was a genius," I replied, not getting through.

"Does he draw?"

"No."

"Well, what good is he?"

I was dumbfounded. Having been raised in a hogan, with little contact with the Indian reservation, he didn't know who Walt Disney was. Such is fame!

We did several pictures, slide films, and so on, over six or seven months, until the grant money for the project ran out. Had we been able to continue the program, it could have opened the gates for other talented underprivileged groups. Certainly it was a constructive and successful experiment. The good news is that such programs seem tailor-made for the present political environment, and we are once again putting together a proposal for an enhanced but similar project for the Indians and other minority groups.

Kids today don't get the chances we did when we started out working for Disney's and other studios. Now, it seems, everyone is satisfied with mediocrity and the status quo. I'm damned mad and so are a few others, but all we can do is try, and somewhere along the line, somebody may reestablish a sense of development before this whole animation business goes down the drain and becomes a lost art. God knows there is still worldwide interest in the medium, but there is no one to lead the way as Disney's once did.

193

People bitten by the animation bug all seem to have the resilience to bounce back and keep trying, no matter how many ups and downs they go through. Most of the men and women in animation have been in it most of their lives and don't like the idea of retiring.

People like Grim Natwick, now somewhere between 95 and 100, keep on flipping, as do Art Babbitt, Hugh Fraser, Phil Duncan, Dick Kelsey, Chuck Couch, Jack Cutting, Chuck Jones, Friz Freleng, Bill Hanna, Joe Barbera, Rudy Zamora, and many more.

Even the second generation is helping to keep the lightboards lit. Young people around the world are trying to recapture this form of entertainment, but alas, it is a hard struggle, the big cop-out being that animation is too expensive. Well, what isn't?

Somewhere there must be someone with the imagination to follow in the footsteps of the early pioneers, guys like Winsor McCay, J. Stuart Blackston, Pat Sullivan, Paul Terry, Max Fleischer, Walter Lantz, and Walt Disney, who all left their indelible marks. But whoever they are, they will still need others who are blessed with enough craziness and talent to create great stories and follow through with great art to produce that finished blend of ideas and craftsmanship.

Looking back, my ride on the roller coaster was at least interesting. I may not be considered a huge success, but I'm still trying. My son Mike and I have come up with a new idea for a picture titled *Our Fabulous World of Fun, Fact, and Fantasy*. With a little bit of luck, maybe we can grab the brass ring and go for another ride.

TICKLEY TICKLEY

ANIMATION WORLD

Way back in the Preface, I mentioned that I'd decided to start this book on the very night my buddy and Disney cohort, Roy Williams, found his waterfall burning down. It was on that historic night that I realized what a lot of crazy things had happened to those of us in the animation game.

It seems that Roy, being the aesthete he was, hated the sight of telephone poles, particularly in his backyard—a backyard he had made into a Polynesian paradise, complete with a free-form swimming pool, tiki lamps, rope, cork and glass floats, woodcarvings, rattan chairs and sofas, and a barbecue cabana strung with nets, built so that the roof dripped into his pool. The vegetation was tropical, too—banana trees, bamboo, vines, ferns, and exotic plants. The works. Then there was that gawdamned ugly telephone pole! He tried growing eucalyptus trees to hide the eyesore, but they also interfered with the telephone wires so much that an all-seeing telephone maintenance crew kept cutting them down.

Then one day Roy came up with the solution: a sixty-foot volcanic waterfall.

Roy enlisted the help of the Disneyland planners, who told him how to construct such an edifice. Gathering scrap lumber, chicken wire, and pipe, Roy built a framework to sustain his mountain, complete with pumps to lift water to the top for his cascade. Of course, Roy did all of the construction himself, including the electrical wiring.

The front of the waterfall was modeled after the genuine Krakatoa, but with hidden colored lights shining on the streams of water coursing down its slopes and spattering into the pool.

All agreed that this South Seas setting was indeed restful, except a few neighbors up and down the block who took umbrage at Roy's luaus and barbecues when they went on till three o'clock in the morning.

Some even complained that the rear view of the waterfall lacked the aesthetic qualities of the other side. This is somewhat understandable, since it was an open construction, akin to the rear end of a movie set.

Of course, Roy paid no attention to these malcontents. As a result, when newly invited friends would ask for his address, veteran guests would explain that they didn't need an address. The Williams house was the only one on the block without a "For Sale" sign.

The parties went on until one wintery night when Roy was fast asleep, and the unmistakable sound of many sirens interrupted him. Firemen and fire equipment were soon invading his backyard.

"My God!" yelled Roy. "Ethel . . . our waterfall's on fire!"

Ethel, a sound sleeper, was aroused. Sleepily she agreed that Roy was indeed correct. The waterfall *was* on fire. Brave firefighters quickly quelled the blaze, but not until Mount Williams was reduced to a huge pile of smoldering debris, much of it hissing in Roy's pool.

Always the genial hosts, Roy and Ethel invited the crew for cake and coffee, while a disturbed neighborhood returned to the comfort of their beds.

Naturally, Roy rebuilt his waterfall. I'd like to think that maybe the animation game can patch up its fall, too.

Epilogue

It was a lovely spring evening in Paris. Roy Disney, Sr., and Jack Cutting had just finished a fine dinner and were taking a stroll. They talked of various subjects related to the studio, mixed with general small talk. They were relaxed and in a reminiscent mood, and finally Jack asked, "Roy, now that Walt is gone, why don't you take some of the credit for the development of the studio since the early days?" Roy stopped Jack with a hand on his arm and said, "Let me tell you a story. When Walt and I first started in business, we had a little studio on Vermont Avenue— really a storefront, with a gold-leaf sign on the front window reading 'Disney Brothers Productions.' As we prospered, we needed larger quarters and we found them in a building on Hyperion Avenue, close to our original store. One evening when Walt and I were discussing our move, Walt said to me, 'Roy, when we move to Hyperion, I'm going to have a large neon sign erected, reading "Walt Disney Studios, Home of Mickey Mouse and Silly Symphonies." He looked at me as if expecting an argument. I said, 'If that's the way you want it.' And Walt said, 'That's the way I want it and that's the way it will be!' And that's the way it was. So you see, Jack, I think it's a little late now, and besides, that's the way Walt would have wanted it."

Roy shrugged and they continued walking.

About the Author

Jack Kinney began working for Walt Disney in 1931 as an inbetween-er and stayed for nearly twenty-seven years. As an animator, story man, and director, he contributed to eleven Disney features and hundreds of shorts, including a series of how-to Goofy shorts beginning with *How to Ride a Horse*. After leaving Disney, Kinney directed *1,001 Arabian Nights,* starring Mr. Magoo, for UPA, and went on to produce and direct more than 100 Popeye shorts for King Features and dozens of TV shows, documentaries, pilots, training films, and commercials for his own company, Jack Kinney Productions.

A partial list of screen credits:

Features
Pinocchio (1940)
Dumbo (1941)
Reluctant Dragon (1941)
Victory Through Air Power (1943)
Saludos Amigos (1943)
Three Caballeros (1945)
Make Mine Music (1946)
Fun and Fancy Free (1947)
Melody Time (1948)
The Adventures of Ichabod and Mr. Toad (1949)
Peter Pan (1953)

Shorts
How to Ride a Horse (1941, Eastman Kodak Award)
Der Fuhrer's Face (1943, Academy Award)
How to Play Football (1944, Academy Award nomination)
Motormania (1950, National Safety Council Award)
Pigs is Pigs (1954, Academy Award nomination)

Notes on the Characters

ED AARDAL Ed, a specialist in effects animation, worked on Goofy shorts and major features such as *Pinocchio* and *Fantasia*. He also put his talents to work for Kling, Era Productions, Hanna-Barbera, DePatie-Freleng, Filmation, and Sanrio.

BILL ABBOTT Bill headed up special effects at 20th Century-Fox.

TOM ADAIR Tom wrote lyrics for Disney films such as *Sleeping Beauty* and *Third Man on the Mountain* and did free-lance work of all kinds.

HAL ADLEQUIST Hal reportedly left the industry after Kinney-Adlequist dissolved.

ELWYN AMBROSE Elwyn was a truly magnificent puppeteer. I lost track of him after our Marcel Marceau project fell through.

FRED "TEX" AVERY Fred moved to Hollywood from Texas in 1928, adopted the name "Tex," and got a job at the Mintz studio. There he embarked on a career which took him to Universal, Warner Brothers, MGM, and Walter Lantz. A truly innovative talent, Tex created such famed characters as Bugs Bunny and Daffy Duck and directed several award-winning TV commercials.

ART BABBITT A talented animator, Art began at Terrytoons in 1929. During the course of his career, he moved on to Disney, UPA, Quartet films (where he was president and cofounder), Hanna-Barbera, and Richard Williams.

JIM BACKUS Jim did the voice of Mr. Magoo and other characters and took part in many radio dramas. Also a film actor, he played Thurston Howell III on "Gilligan's Island."

RALPH BAKSHI A producer of controversial, avant-garde animated films, Ralph Bakshi began his career in New York, working at Terrytoons and Famous Studio before moving to Hollywood. His cartoon feature *Fritz the Cat*, released in 1971, was rated X. The producer's current work includes "Mighty Mouse: The New Adventure," a TV series for children.

MIKE BALUKAS Mike was a deaf and dumb animator from New York City, where, in the 1920s, he had been a painter on Krazy Kat for Charles Mintz.

JOE BARBERA A graduate of New York University and the American Banking Institute, Joe was a banker until his success in free-lance cartooning led him to change careers. After working as an animator at Van Beuren, he took a job at MGM in Hollywood. There, he met Bill Hanna, with whom he formed Hanna-Barbera studio in 1957. Among their first-rate cartoons are over 160 Tom and Jerry shorts, "The Flintstones," and "The Jetsons."

DON BARCLAY Don, a versatile artist and comedian, did voices for *Pinocchio, Cinderella, Alice in Wonderland,* and *Mary Poppins,* among others.

CARL BARKS A prolific Disney story man, Carl wrote many of the Donald Duck comic books between 1942 and 1966. During this period he created Scrooge McDuck.

BOB BEEMILLER Bob worked in my Goofy unit. From 1935 on, he was an animator at nearly fifteen different studios, including Mintz, Fleischer, MGM, Lantz, Sutherland, Disney, DePatie-Frelang, Filmation, Christian Mission Films, Hanna-Barbera, and the March of Dimes.

AL BERTINO Al, a member of Disney's Story Department, had also worked at WED (the Disneyland operation), Mintz, Harman-Ising, UPA, Snowball, and Grantray-Lawrence.

TOM BLACKBURN The author of many Western novels, Tom wrote the screenplay and co-wrote lyrics for Disney's two *Davy Crockett* films.

J. STUART BLACKTON J. Stuart Blackton, thought to be the first American animator, released *Thief on the Roof* in 1897. He also invented the Vitagraph camera for trick photography.

BILLY BLETCHER A little man with a big voice, Billy did voices for Pegleg Pete, the Big Bad Wolf, and many other animated characters of the thirties.

STEVE BOSUSTOW Steve worked for Ub Iwerks, Walter Lantz, and Disney before pioneering new animation techniques as president of UPA in *Gerald McBoing Boing* and the Mr. Magoo cartoons.

HAZEL AND LILY BOUNDS Both inkers, Lily married Walt Disney and Hazel married Bill Cottrell, Disney's first cameraman.

JACK BOYD Jack left Disney to form his own studio. When it didn't work out, he came back to Disney and was named head of the Effects Animation.

HOMER BRIGHTMAN A story man, Homer was the subject of some of our best practical jokes. He left Disney in the late forties to work for MGM and Lantz. He also wrote for live-action TV.

SUE BRISTOL Sue ran the Ink and Paint Department and much of the studio social scene as well.

AL BRODAX Al, who worked with King Features, produced *The Yellow Submarine.*

STUART BUCHANAN A talent scout, Stuart also worked on pictures. He did the voice of Humbert in *Snow White.*

PETE BURNESS Pete joined Van Beuren in about 1934 as an animator while still in his twenties. He worked at Warner Brothers briefly in the late forties before joining UPA to direct the Magoo series. Two of his Magoo films—*When Magoo Flew* (1945) and *Magoo's Puddle Jumper* (1956)—won Academy Awards.

BRUCE BUSHMAN Bruce did layout for the "Nutcracker Suite" sequence in *Fantasia* and was a sketch artist for *20,000 Leagues under the Sea.*

CHARLEY BYRNES Charley moved from New York to animate for Disney in the early days of expansion. He also did layout.

WALTER CATLETT The voice of the fox in *Pinocchio,* Walter was also a popular comedian and actor in films like *Bringing Up Baby.*

FRANK CHURCHILL Frank, who was already at Disney when I arrived, composed the famous Depression song "Who's Afraid of the Big Bad Wolf?" He also wrote the music for many other Disney hits, including the soundtrack of *Snow White,* and won an Academy Award for his accomplishments.

LES CLARK An early recruit to the Disney Studio, Les's native artistic talent and superb animation skills led him to become one of Walt's "nine old men." At retirement, he was the senior Disney employee.

TOM CODRICK Tom worked on many major films as a Disney layout man in the thirties and forties, including *Snow White, Bambi,* and *Fantasia.*

PINTO COLVIG A circus clown and one of the original Keystone Kops, Pinto Colvig played clarinet and ocarina. He was also a story man and did the voices of Goofy, Pluto, Grumpy, and various insect creatures.

BOB COOK As an engineer Bob was responsible for sound recording in many Disney films from the forties through the late sixties.

BILL COTTRELL Bill was known for his good taste as a story man and director and was the first Disney employee to reach fifty-year tenure. He married Walt's sister-in-law and was Disney's first cameraman.

CHUCK COUCH Chuck began in 1929 at Disney as an assistant animator, then became an animator and story man. He later worked for Mintz, Lantz, MGM, and Hanna-Barbera and opened his own studio.

ART CRUICKSHANK After leaving Disney, Art worked as a cameraman and in special effects at 20th Century-Fox.

JACK CUTTING Jack began as an inker, worked his way up to animator, and became Disney's first assistant director. A diplomat and peacemaker, he moved swiftly into international management when Disney expanded into worldwide distribution of feature films. He was well liked by both Walt and Roy Disney.

JOE D'IGALO Joe was an effects animator who moved from New York during the early Disney expansion. He animated for Schlesinger in the late thirties.

UGO D'ORSI A very thorough effects animator with a strong Italian accent, Ugo worked on *Fantasia, Snow White,* and other films.

ELIOT DANIEL Eliot was an Academy Award–winning musician on the original *Peter Pan* crew. He also composed music for Bongo in *Fun and Fancy Free.* Other credits include *Song of the South, Melody Time,* and *So Dear to My Heart.*

KEN DARBY Ken became a musical director at 20th Century-Fox, where he worked on *Camelot* and other pictures. At Disney he worked on *Song of the South, Melody Time, So Dear to My Heart,* and *The Adventures of Ichabod and Mr. Toad.*

MARC DAVIS Marc, a top animator at Disney for more than forty years, was one of Walt's "nine old men." He created many great characters from Bambi and Thumper to Cruella De Vil in *101 Dalmations.* He also created many of Disneyland's three-dimensional attractions and taught art part time at Chouinard for seventeen years.

GILLES ARMAND RENE de TREMAUDAN Known as "Frenchy," Gilles became an animator, story man, and, finally, a priest.

LOU DEBNEY Assistant director on *Pinocchio,* when the picture was finished, Lou remained at Disney, where he worked on *Perri, Sign of Zorro,* and *Adventures of Bullwhip Griffin,* which was released in 1967.

MERRILL DeMARIS A story department writer, Merrill worked on *Snow White* and other major films.

DAVID H. DePATIE The son of well-known animation pioneer Edmond DePatie, David headed the Warner Brothers cartoon department during its last few years before it closed in 1963.

PHIL DIKE Phil was an illustrator who taught with Don Graham and an expert on color and color film. He later moved near the beach in Southern California and became nationally famous for his watercolors. At Disney he did backgrounds for *Snow White,* story development for *Fantasia,* and color consulting for *The Three Caballeros.*

RAY DISNEY Ray ran an insurance company back East before moving to Hollywood.

ROY DISNEY Walt's brother Roy was a financial wizard who kept the company going despite hard times and Walt's extravagance. His son, Roy Junior, plays a large role in the contemporary Walt Disney Company.

GEORGE DRAKE George helped Walt recruit New Yorkers during the mid-1930s. Later he became studio manager. He was related by marriage to Ben Sharpsteen.

PHIL DUNCAN Phil, a talented animator, worked on *Bambi* and other Disney movies, then became a free-lancer after the strike. He also worked at Screen Gems.

EARL DUVALL A story man, Earl quit Disney under duress. Later he directed briefly for Schlesinger.

CLIFF EDWARDS In addition to being the voice of Jiminy Cricket in *Pinocchio*, Cliff sang "When You Wish Upon a Star" and "Give a Little Whistle" in the film. While with Ziegfield, he was known as "Ukelele Ike," and he made many records and was a national favorite in the days of acoustic recordings.

IRA ENGLANDER Ira was the successful producer of animated and live-action educational films and of entertainment films such as *Running Brave* and *Puss 'n' Boots*. He is also an attorney. (No relation to Otto Englander.)

OTTO ENGLANDER A longtime story many at Disney, Otto worked on *Pinocchio* and other major films. He also worked on *Puss 'n' Boots* and *Jack and the Beanstalk* at Ub Iwerks studio.

ANDY ENGMAN Andy, who began his career as a Disney animator in 1934, received a Golden Globe award for fifty years in animation. His credits include *Make Mine Music* and *Saludos Amigos*.

AL EUGSTER Al started as an inker for Pat Sullivan, moved to Max Fleisher's studio in 1930 as an inbetweener, then moved to Mintz and on to Ub Iwerks. He was an animator with Iwerks until 1935, when he joined Disney. Four years later he became head animator at Famous Studios (Paramount), where he stayed for more than twenty-five years.

NORM FERGUSON Norm arrived at Disney as an animator in 1929, and his revolutionary style still influences the industry. Norm, considered the fastest animator in the business, was directing animator on nine famous Disney features between 1937 and 1953, and between 1930 and 1954, he animated more than seventy-five shorts.

MARY FLANIGAN Loved by everyone, Mary turned a former broom closet into a snack shop and became the studio bookie.

MAX FLEISCHER Max and his brother Dave produced animated cartoons such as *Out of the Inkwell* as early as 1916 in their New York studio. Two of his characters—Betty Boop and Popeye—brought him fame.

EMIL FLOHRI Emil spent most of his career as art editor of *Life* magazine before coming to Disney. He retired when he left the studio and spent his time painting.

HUGH FRASER A top Disney animator (and pal of Bing Crosby), Hugh counts *Pinocchio, Fantasia, Dumbo,* and *Lady and the Tramp* among his credits. He also worked for Hanna-Barbera and Format.

FRIZ FRELANG Friz began his animation career in Kansas City in 1924, then worked for Disney on *Oswald, the Lucky Rabitt* in 1926. In 1932, he went to Warner Brothers, where he stayed for the next thirty-two years. The creator of *The Pink Panther,* he won five Academy Awards.

BERNARD GARBUTT Bernard worked briefly as a teacher with Don Graham. He was an animator on *Bambi,* and later worked for Walter Lantz.

BILL GARITY Bill, who became head of the Disney engineering department, developed a camera and stereo system for *Fantasia*. Later, he became production manager for Walter Lantz. Bill got his start at Pat Powers's company, which provided Disney's first sound system.

MARCELLITE GARNER An early voice talent, Marcellite did Minnie Mouse. She was also an inker.

HAZEL GEORGE Hazel was the company nurse. She relayed studio gossip and was Walt's confidant and advisor, especially in his latter days.

CLYDE "GERRY" GERONIMI Clyde, an early animator and director, worked for Bray in New York in the 1920s before moving to Hollywood. He directed for Disney until the late fifties or early sixties.

BURTON (BERT) GILLETT Bert worked as an animator at Hearst International until it closed in 1921. In 1929, he became Disney's second director. He then returned to New York to work for Van Beuren (which folded after he left), and in 1938 returned to Hollywood to work for Walter Lantz.

DON GRAHAM An art teacher for many years, Don was commissioned by Walt to conduct evening classes in 1932. He remained at Disney until 1955, leaving only for the duration of World War II. He then returned to his alma mater, Chouinard, where he ultimately became chairman of the faculty.

JOE GRANT Joe began his career as a newspaper caricaturist, moved to Disney to draw animated caricatures of celebrities for *Mickey's Gala Premiere,* and stayed on as a story man, working on *Snow White, Fantasia, Dumbo,* and other features. Later, he headed the Disney Model Department. After nineteen years at Disney, he left to pursue independent art projects.

DON GRIFFITH Don did layout on my first short, *Bone Trouble,* and on many major Disney features, including *Victory Through Air Power, Cinderella, Alice in Wonderland,* and *101 Dalmations*.

MITCH HAMILBURG Mitch, my agent, was also agent to Will Rogers, Gene Autry, and other well-known personalities.

ROLLIN "HAM" HAMILTON Another of the animators who moved from Kansas City to L.A. with Walt, "Ham" had already left by the time I arrived. He became a top animator at Schlesinger in the thirties.

DAVE HAND Dave began a pioneering career in animation, starting with the creation of the cartoon character Andy Gump in 1919. He animated and directed for Fleischer Studio, made some films for Kodak, and then joined Disney as an animator in 1930, making about three dozen shorts before moving into direction. In the 1940s, he was recruited by J. Arthur Rank in England, a company that hoped to compete with Disney. After years with Rank, Hand produced many films on his own.

BILL HANNA Bill began his career submitting story ideas to studios, then was hired by MGM as an animation director. There, he met Joe Barbera, and together they created the Tom and Jerry series, which won seven Oscars in twenty years. In 1957, this successful team formed their own studio, Hanna-Barbera.

LEIGH HARLINE Leigh, originally a radio organist, wrote the music for *Snow White* and *Pinocchio*. He later moved on to MGM and composed many live-action scores.

HUGH HARMAN Hugh worked briefly with Walt in Kansas City. After producing two pictures there, he joined Disney in Los Angeles in 1925. In 1928, he and Rudolph Ising (who had arrived at Disney concurrently) formed a company that produced Looney Tunes and Merrie Melodies for Warner Brothers. From 1934 to 1938 the team produced cartoons for MGM, which both men later joined. In 1941, Hugh became an independent producer.

CHUCK HAWES Chuck was a film editor—and later an independent editor and cameraman.

T. HEE T. Hee, first a caricaturist at MGM and Hal Roach, joined Warner Brothers in 1936, then moved to Disney, where he became a writer, designer, and director. He later held similar responsibilities at UPA and taught at several prominent art schools.

ART HEINEMAN Noted for his well-conceived layouts, Heineman designed the main bug characters in Walter Lantz's *Enemy Bacteria* and gave Woody Woodpecker a new color scheme. He also worked at several other studios, including UPA and Warner Brothers.

HUGH HENNESY A layout man with outstanding artistic talent, Hugh's credits include *Snow White, Pinocchio,* and *Fantasia,* among others.

BILL HERWIG A true eccentric, Bill quit the business and went to the South Seas. After years of traveling, he married a talented Mexican woman and settled in the Southwest.

CAL HOWARD Cal joined me for Popeye productions after stints at Lantz, Iwerks, Warner Brothers, Screen Gems, Fleischer, MGM, and Disney. He was a capable story and gag man.

JOHN HUBLEY John, a layout man at Disney, left the studio as a result of the strike and became one of the key animators at United Productions of America (UPA). In 1952, he formed his own studio, Storyboard, Inc., to produce commercials. With his wife, Faith, he has produced numerous important films, including three Academy Award winners.

DICK HUEMER Dick, an early animator from New York, joined Disney in 1934, where he worked on *Fantasia, Dumbo,* and *Alice in Wonderland.* He was also a director and writer.

KEN HULTGREN Ken joined my Popeye group as an animator. At Disney, he had animated *Bambi* and *Sleeping Beauty.*

EARL HURD Although technically in the Story Department, Earl could do everything. He held many patents on animation processes, including the technique of cels, the celluloid overlays used to avoid retracing backgrounds. His career began in 1917 when he and pioneer J.R. Bray formed the Bray-Hurd company.

ALBERT HURTER A story man and native Australian, Albert worked in early animation studios, including Raoul Barre's, before arriving at Disney. He had a rare talent for inspiring animators with his wonderful ideas and drawing ability.

RUDOLPH ISING Ising began animating for Walt Disney in 1921 and moved to L.A., along with Hugh Harman, to join Disney in 1925. After leaving Disney, he created the character Fumble for "Football Forecasts," one of the first TV shows combining animation with live action, and won an Academy Award for his 1941 cartoon *The Milky Way.* (Also see Hugh Harman.)

UB IWERKS Ub worked closely with Walt in Kansas City, producing the first Disney films. He then joined Walt in Hollywood as his first animator. Ub left in 1930 to open his own studio, but he returned to Disney in 1940. He often designed and built his own equipment.

WILFRED JACKSON Although Wilfred began work at Disney as an unpaid helper in 1928, his extraordinary creativity quickly led him to become Walt's first director. He adapted sound to animation in *Steamboat Willie,* starring Mickey Mouse, putting the Disney studio at least a year ahead of competitors. He directed three Academy Award-winning shorts, and retired from Disney in 1961.

GUS JEKEL Gus started at Disney in the traffic department, and became an animator before moving on to TV production and live-action directing. He founded FilmFair studio in 1960 and has produced many award-winning live and animated films.

CARL JOHNSON Our trainer in the Penthouse Club at Disney, Carl had been the Swedish wrestling champ in the 1912 Olympics.

OLLIE JOHNSTON Ollie was hired by Disney in 1935 and retired in 1978 as supervising animator. One of Walt's "nine old men," he worked on all Disney features except *Dumbo* and has coauthored several books on animation with his lifelong friend, colleague, and neighbor, Frank Thomas.

CHUCK JONES Chuck began as a cel washer at UB Iwerks studio in 1931, then went to Warner Brothers. There he worked as a director and created many characters including Road Runner. Later, after a stint at MGM, he became an independent producer of many prime-time TV specials. He is the recipient of three Oscars, a Peabody, an Annie, the CINE, two Reubens, and several other awards.

DICKEY JONES A typical spoiled child actor, Dickey did the voice of Pinocchio at age four.

ISHAM JONES Isham was a big-band leader and popular musician of my youth.

VOLUS JONES Volus, starting in 1934, worked for Columbia, Disney, UPA, Bakshi-Krantz, Hanna-Barbera, and Screen Gems as an animator.

CHARLEY JUDELS Charley did the voices for the Evil Coachman and Stromboli in *Pinocchio,* as well as for characters in many other features and shorts.

BILL JUSTICE An innovative animator and director, Bill worked on *Fantasia, Bambi,* and other films well into the fifties. Later, he turned his talents to exhibit design for Disneyland.

MILT KAHL A top-notch animator and one of Walt's "nine old men," Milt joined Disney in 1934 and stayed more than forty years, working on twenty-three shorts and twenty-three features during that period. He was married to Walt's niece.

RAY KELLY Ray, a story man, worked at Van Beuren Studio in New York before he joined Disney in Hollywood. He left after a few years to become a priest.

DICK KELSEY Dick, one of Disneyland's designers, was an excellent layout and background artist. His fine art has been displayed in many museums, and he has sold hundreds of greeting card illustrations.

TOM KENNINGTON A writer and exnewspaperman, Tom worked with me teaching animation to Navajo kids. He had a gift for humor, and entertained us for hours with stories about his years working for notorius film actess Marion Davies and her seafaring husband.

WARD KIMBALL Ward, a top animator, went directly from art school to Disney as an apprentice animator and became full animator in 1936. One of Walt's "nine old men," he remained at Disney throughout his animation career until 1973.

HAL KING An animator from New York, Hal worked on many Disney films, from *The Three Caballeros* in the mid-forties through *The Jungle Book* in the late sixties.

JACK KING Jack learned his trade with Hearst and J.R. Bray in New York. He was recruited by Disney around 1929, left to direct for Schlesinger in the mid-thirties, then returned to Disney for ten years to direct a new Donald Duck series. He also worked for Warner Brothers.

DICK KINNEY My brother Dick, a Disney story man, worked on Scrooge McDuck, among other characters. He also worked at UPA and free-lanced comic books.

JANE KINNEY My wife Jane started her career at Disney in research and development and eventually became my assistant director on *Bambi, Victory Through Air Power, The Wind in the Willows,* and other projects. She worked in television after leaving the studio.

MIKE KINNEY My son Mike worked with me on Popeye and other projects as a cameraman and editor. He is currently free-lancing.

GEORGE LANE An animator, George left Disney early, and that was the last I heard of him.

WALTER LANTZ Walter started his working life as a copyboy for a New York newspaper at age fifteen. He then joined an early New York studio to draw Katzenjammer Kids, Krazy Kat, and other cartoons. In 1922, he became a producer for J.R. Bray, making films such as *Col. Heeza Liar.* He went to Hollywood in 1926, joined Universal in 1928, and operated his own Hollywood studio for many years. During the course of his career, he created Woody Woodpecker, Andy Panda, and other classic cartoon characters. His wife Gracie does Woody's voice.

RUDY LARRIVA Rudy's animation career began in 1937 and took him to Warner Brothers, Disney, UPA, Format, Filmation, Sutherland, and Hanna-Barbera. He worked on *Song of the South* and *Melody Time* while at Disney and was a member of my Popeye group.

ERIC LARSON Eric started at Disney in 1933 and was still working there fifty years later. A fine animator, he created a program to recruit and train talented young people to carry on the Disney tradition. He was one of Walt's "nine old men."

RICO LeBRUN Rico, an art teacher, worked with Don Graham instructing animators at Disney. He later became involved with character development for animals in *Bambi.*

GUNTHER LESSING Gunther represented Pancho Villa, the Mexican revolutionary leader, before he was hired as the studio attorney in the early thirties. He was little liked by most of the staff at Disney. After his unsuccessful handling of the strike in 1941, Walt demoted him.

BERT LEWIS Bert, originally from Kansas City, was one of the three musicians at Disney when I arrived. He later became the first music director at MGM's cartoon studio.

JOHN LOUNSBERY John spent almost forty years at Disney and was one of Walt's "nine old men." He was animator or directing animator on twenty-five features, from *Snow White* in 1937 to *The Many Adventures of Winnie the Pooh* in 1977, and he animated almost as many shorts within those years.

ED LOVE An animator, Ed started his career in 1930 at Disney, where he worked on *Fantasia*. He later moved on to Lantz, MGM, and Hanna-Barbera.

JIM LOWERRE A Disney engineer, Jim did sound and cutting. Walt got his first lesson in using a camera from Jim Lowerre back at the Kansas City Film Ad Company.

KEN LOWMAN Ken was a Disney musician and also wrote and recorded the music for many of my Popeye shorts.

HAM LUSKE A business major at the University of California, Ham began work at Disney in 1931. He spent over thirty-five years at the studio, where he became both a director and one of Walt's favorite animators, playing a major role in over fifteen features and forty shorts.

DAN MACMANUS A dedicated effects animator, Dan worked on *Bambi* and other features. He was a good polo player and a big asset to Walt's polo team.

CARLOS MANRIQUEZ A great athlete, Carlos had more brothers than we could keep track of. The brothers had their own baseball team, the Mexican Manglers, and were always tough to beat. Carlos eventually moved to Mexico and opened his own studio.

JOSH MEADOR Josh, an effects animator and painter, worked on many films including *Snow White, Fantasia,* and *The Reluctant Dragon.*

WINSOR McCAY Winsor was a newspaper cartoonist who turned animator in the early 1900s. His 1914 film *Gertie the Dinosaur* showed that animated cartoons could be true works of art and made him a respected industry figure.

JUANITA McCLURG Juanita joined my Popeye group as a checker. She also worked on *Puss 'n' Boots* and on Bakshi's *Fritz the Cat.*

BOB McCORMICK Bob worked as checker and assistant director at Disney.

JOHN McLEISH John did the voice of Goofy for me at Disney, as well as many other characters at New York studios. He was also a story man.

JOHN McMANUS An effects animator, John came to Disney from New York, stayed a few years, and then went back.

BILL MELENDEZ At Disney Bill animated on *Dumbo, Bambi, Fantasia,* and other films. He opened his own studio in Hollywood in 1964 and another in London in 1970. Now Bill animates the television Snoopy specials.

FRED MOORE Freddie joined Disney in 1930 and quickly rose to animator. Although his only prior experience had been entering drawing contests, the charm of his work soon markedly influenced the studio's drawing style. He contributed to many Disney features but is perhaps best known for his dwarfs in *Snow White.*

LARRY MOREY Larry was a songwriter for *Snow White* and *Bambi.* He left Disney to work for the Ice Capades.

KEN MUSE Starting in 1937, Ken animated at Disney, Hanna-Barbera, and as a free-lancer. He also worked on Tom and Jerry cartoons at MGM for many years.

MIKE MYERS A New Yorker, Mike left Disney after his stint in the Story Department and returned to the East, and that's the last I heard of him.

CLARENCE NASH Clarence was doing bird and animal imitations for an L.A. talent company in 1934 when Walt heard him and decided he might be the right voice for Disney's new Donald Duck character. Walt's hunch proved correct. Nash did all of Donald's voices, even those in foreign languages, until his death in 1985.

GRIM NATWICK Grim is one of the grand old men of the animation business. Many great animators at Disney and elsewhere learned their skills under his tutelage. He won the prestigious Winsor McCay Award in 1975 and was well past ninety when he agilely mounted the stage in 1984 to present an Annie Award to a London colleague.

ED NOFZIGER Ed joined my Popeye group as a gag man. He did free-lance stories for me and free-lance comic books for Disney, and was a prolific magazine cartoonist.

LESTER NOVROS Lester worked on *Fantasia* at Disney, then became executive director of production and president of Graphic Films Corp., notable for creating motion pictures for world fairs and exhibits.

MARION O'CALLAHAN Bill Hanna's sister, Marion did ink and paint for Disney and UPA, then opened her own free-lance ink and paint service.

DEAN AND GLEN OLSON My two buddies from the *Los Angeles Herald Examinor,* Dean and Glen started an egg farm that became Olson Industries, whose stock is now traded internationally.

FRANK OREB Frank worked on many pictures including the "All the Cats Join In" sequence in *Make Mine Music.* He was also a fine artist and eventually left the business to paint.

AMBROSIA PALIWODA Ambrosia started his animation career in 1933 and worked at Disney, Hanna-Barbera, Filmation, and Duck Soup. He did character animation on *101 Dalmations*.

TOM PALMER A New york director hired from Van Beuren Studios during the first Disney expansion wave, Palmer was later one of the first directors at the Schlesinger (Warner Brothers) cartoon studio.

RAY PATIN Ray was a Disney animator and later opened his own studio.

PERCE PEARCE Perce once ghosted the comic strip *The Captain and the Kids*. Later he was sent to England by Walt to direct live action films.

BILL PEET Bill started as a Disney inbetweener in 1937 but soon moved to the Story Department, where his first assignment was on *Pinocchio*. He also worked on story and design for *101 Dalmations, Cinderella,* and *Sleeping Beauty*. Bill, who stayed at Disney until 1964, was also a prolific and popular author of children's books.

CHARLIE PHILLIPPI As a layout man, Charlie was one of the best in handling color, although he once told me in confidence that he was color-blind. He worked on many films, including *Pinocchio,* and stayed at Disney for his entire career.

FRANK POWERS Irishman Frank Powers and I were both hired as inbetweeners in 1931. He went free-lance six months or so later.

FRED QUIMBY Fred became head of the young MGM animation studio in 1937 and retired almost twenty years later.

JACK REEDER Jack was a manager for Disney. He attended Dartmouth College and brought his school colors with him. He even wore cleats to play in our touch football games.

HARRY REEVES A story man, Harry eventually left Disney, went into business for himself, and made millions.

WOLFGANG REITHERMAN "Woolie" joined Disney in 1933 and became an animator, directing animator, and director. When Walt died in 1966, Reitherman succeeded him as producer. One of Walt's "nine old men," he had a major influence on more than twenty features and many shorts.

CHARLIE RIVERS Charlie was a bootlegger who operated a local blind pig. We lost track of him after Prohibition was repealed.

BILL ROBERTS A director, animator, and a very good businessman, Bill left Disney to go into real estate and construction, and reportedly became very wealthy.

MISTER ROGERS A Disney maintenance man and carpenter, his first name was Joseph.

DAVE ROSE Another layout man who moved into the story department, Dave worked for me on *Pinocchio*. Later he went to NBC to do publicity.

JOHN ROSE John was an expediter (gofer) for the story department. He later produced a combination live-action and animation film called *The Incredible Mr. Limpet*.

JACK ROURKE Jack scouted voice talent for *Peter Pan*. He has also done narration for documentaries and has participated in many telethons.

CHRISTIAN RUB The voice of Geppetto in *Pinocchio*, Christian frequently did voices of kindly old men for MGM, Fox, and Warner Brothers.

MILT SCHAFFER Milt started animating at Disney in 1933 and moved to the Story Department in 1937, where he worked on many of the great characters: Mickey, Donald, Pluto, and Goofy. In 1954 he left to do television commercials.

RETTA SCOTT Retta, the first woman animator at Disney, worked on *Bambi*. Later she married a submarine captain and retired.

TED SEARS Hired from Max Fleischer in New York as head of the Story Department, Ted was a clever, insouciant, and enjoyable character. He invented the storyboard technique used at Disney for presenting films.

CAROLINE SHAFER Caroline was Walt's secretary for many years and later married the great musician Frank Churchill.

BEN SHARPSTEEN The first animator recruited from New York (in 1929), Ben became a mainstay producer and director. He was a good teacher, especially for inbetweeners and assistants, and had a tremendous background. Between 1916 and 1929 he had worked at Hearst, Terrytoons, and Max Fleischer.

DICK SHAW Dick Shaw was a gag man in the Story Department at Disney. Dick wrote checks for everything; he would never run up a tab.

RICHARD AND ROBERT SHERMAN Brothers Dick and Bob were an extraordinary songwriting team responsible for the scores of many Disney films including *The Jungle Book* and *Mary Poppins*. Several of their songs such as "Spoonful of Sugar" and *"Supercalifragilisticexpialidocious"* are classics.

EVIE SHERWOOD Evie joined me for Popeye productions as a checker. She worked for Disney, UPA, Snowball, Format, Ray Patin, Sutherland, and Hanna-Barbera.

JOHN SIBLEY A great animator, John worked with me on Goofy shorts. He stayed at Disney for his entire career.

PAUL SMITH An innovative musician, Paul Smith worked on *True Life Adventures, Snow White,* and other films. He was a close colleague of Frank Churchill.

WEBB SMITH Webb was a gag man and a great practical joker in the Story Department. After a period of cartooning for Hearst, he stayed with Walt for the remainder of his career.

ED SMITH Ed, an animator, once studied for the priesthood. He left Disney before the strike to do free-lance work.

DON SMITH Don was hired in 1931 the same day I was. He later did layout, then moved on to Harman-Ising.

FRED SPENCER Fred animated Donald Duck shorts and worked on *Snow White*.

CARL STALLING Carl, who moved from Kansas City with Walt, was Disney's first musician, and one of the few musicians to win an Annie Award (1978). For many years, he composed all the scores for Warner Brothers cartoons.

GRACE STANZELL A Disney animator who joined me to animate Popeye, Grace also worked for me on *Puss 'n' Boots*. Later, she worked for Bakshi.

LEOPOLD STOKOWSKI The famous conductor worked with the studio as a consultant on the score of *Fantasia*.

PAT SULLIVAN Pat began as a New York cartoonist in the teens. He produced *Felix the Cat* for Paramount around 1919 and in 1921 opened his own New York studio.

HOWARD SWIFT I worked with Howard on many pictures at Disney. A superb and swift animator, he created the imaginative pink elephant sequence in *Dumbo*. He liked fast boats and cars and commuted from Ojai to the Disney studio in his own plane. After leaving Disney, he directed at Screen Gems and formed his own TV commercial studio.

GUSTAVE TENGGREN Gustave was a fine illustrator brought in early in the development of *Pinocchio* to help the story men create mood.

PAUL TERRY Paul and his brother John owned a New York studio that served as a training ground for many talented animators.

FRANK THOMAS A Disney animator from 1934 until 1978, Thomas became supervising animator, creating memorable scenes in *Snow White, Bambi, Lady and the Tramp,* and many other films. He was the head of the Air Force Animation Unit during World War II. One of Walt's "nine old men," he also wrote books with his longtime colleague and fellow Stanford alumnus, Ollie Johnston.

RILEY THOMPSON Riley animated Mickey Mouse cartoons and other short subjects and eventually left Disney to free-lance. He was a good friend of Freddie Moore.

HARVEY TOOMBS Harvey was a Disney animator who later worked with me at UPA and on Popeye for King Features.

BILL TYTLA Bill, one of Disney's top animators, worked on *Snow White, Fantasia, Dumbo,* and other films. He joined Disney in 1934 after working sporadically for the Terry brothers in New York. He left Disney after the strike in 1941.

HARRY TYTLE A unit manager and an "umbrella man" for Walt, Harry was studio rep on *Almost Angels,* filmed offshore in the early 1960s.

LAURIE VEJAR Laurie was a free-lance film editor for Disney and other studios.

EVELYN VENABLE Evelyn did the voice of the Blue Fairy in *Pinocchio*. She was also an actress in live-action pictures.

OLLIE WALLACE A musician and composer, Ollie wrote music for *Dumbo, Ichabod Crane,* and other films during his many years at Disney.

COTTON WARBURTON As an editor, Cotton won an Academy Award for his work on *Mary Poppins*. He was an All-American football player at the University of Southern California.

NED WASHINGTON Ned was a musician and lyricist for *Snow White, Dumbo, Pinocchio,* and other films.

CLAIR WEEKS Clair began animating Disney films in the mid-thirties and stayed for many years. Later she went to India, where her father had been a missionary, to teach animation.

RICHARD WILLIAMS Richard's studio in London released its first major animated film, *The Little Island,* in 1958. Many great Disney animators, including Grim Natwick and Art Babbitt, have worked and taught at Williams's studio.

ROY WILLIAMS Roy followed the same career path I did at Disney, going from inbetweener to animator to story man. Then he became the head Mouseketeer on "The Mickey Mouse Show." Roy also published his cartoons in *The New Yorker* and dedicated a collection of this work to Walt Disney.

RALPH WOLF Ralph was hired as an inbetweener in 1931 and became an animator and story man. He later moved to Warner Brothers for several years, after which he drew free-lance comic strips. He was in the process of creating a new comic strip when he died at the age of ninety-three.

RALPH WRIGHT Ralph, a gag man, went to England with Dave Hand, but returned to Disney four or five years later. He was a story man on Goofy shorts and *Song of the South*.

CY YOUNG Cy, who spoke with a pronounced Chinese accent, was head of special effects. He came to Disney from the Bray studio in New York, where he had been since 1924.

RUDY ZAMORA Rudy was another animator who moved from Flesicher in New York to join Disney in 1930. After leaving Disney, Rudy moved to other studios: Iwerks, Screen Gems, Walter Lantz, and Hanna-Barbera.